C

MR

D0522670

Someone to Watch Over Me

Someone To Watch Over Me

The True Tale of a Survivor
Haunted by the Demons of Abuse

Izzy Hammond

with Robert Potter

MAINSTREAM
PUBLISHING

EDINBURGH AND LONDON

First published in Great Britain in 2007 by
MAINSTREAM PUBLISHING COMPANY (EDINBURGH) LTD
7 Albany Street
Edinburgh EH1 3UG

ISBN 9781845962586

This book is a work of non-fiction based on the life,
experiences and recollections of Izzy Hammond. All names
of people and places, and some dates, sequences and details
of events have been changed to protect the privacy of others.
The author has stated to the publishers that, except in such
respects, not affecting the substantial accuracy of the work,
the contents of this book are true.

A catalogue record for this book is available
from the British Library.

Typeset in Apollo and Lucinda

Printed in Great Britain by
Cox & Wyman Ltd, Reading

I wish to dedicate this book to the survivors of abuse and rape in recognition of their strength and relentless bravery

———————

Charlie Kothary Potter
Forever now a butterfly

Author's Note

All the names and identities of those who feature in this book have been altered, along with the geographical locations and some dates. I have used a pseudonym to write it. I have done this to protect the anonymity of my children, though they are aware of its publication. The reason for this is that, while I hope telling my story might help others who have found or find themselves in a similar situation, my children and grandchildren have the right to privacy, and I would ask for this to be respected.

Acknowledgements

There are a number of people I would like to thank, the most important one being my husband for his unfailing belief, support and encouragement, and for loving me warts and all.

Thank you to my children, for whom I acknowledge this continues to be a painful journey. You are stronger than you think.

To my mum and dad. Without your love, I wonder how I would have had the strength to survive.

To my soul sisters. Without you both, life would be a much colder place, thank you for always being there.

Thank you to all of my family, near and far, for your constant support, encouragement and belief in what I was doing.

My thanks also to Richard McCann for his help and advice and just for being there for me.

To my dearest friend Joy, you gave me the gift of time to find my way, and I owe you countless boxes of tissues from over the years.

To Caroline, for your friendship, professional eye and the many cups of coffee we've shared.

My heartfelt thanks to Sarah and all of the staff at the Priory Hospital, especially Elaine, who held my hand all of the way and never wavered. Also thank you to Harry for my 'bag of tools', of which I now have many.

My thanks to Bill Campbell, Ailsa Bathgate and the team at Mainstream Publishing for allowing my voice to be heard.

A very special thank you to Robert Potter, who turned my words into book form. Thank you for your sensitivity, perception, patience and continued support. I could not have done this without you.

Contents

The Powder-Blue Coat

Spring 1965

I could hardly contain my excitement as the train pulled in to London's King's Cross station on that bright spring morning. It wasn't just the typical nine year old's thrill at travelling to the big city that fired my enthusiasm, as I'd made the trip with my birth-father Ronald many times before. This time I was wearing my brand-new coat, a beautiful powder-blue one, and I felt so proud as I stepped down from the train and onto the platform. As on previous journeys, I was taking Ronald to the Royal Institute for the Blind on Tottenham Court Road. He worked for them from home as a basket maker. Ronald had been born profoundly deaf and he also suffered from tunnel vision, which meant he had no peripheral vision whatsoever, and a disorder in his middle ear often made him stagger like a drunk. I therefore became his 'eyes and ears' on these trips to the institute's store of weaving supplies, where he used to work before his disabilities made this impossible. As I held firmly onto his arm, I was often pushed off the pavement into the path of oncoming traffic as he veered from side to side.

We made it to the institute in one piece, but the entrance was locked when we arrived. Waiting down a side alley was one of the workers, a woman I'd met before on previous visits with Ronald. This woman had something wrong with her eyes that made her look very strange to me, but she had always been very kind. I never knew her name – no one had ever told me – but she'd sit me on her knee as I enjoyed the drink and biscuits she invariably gave me, all the while running her hand up and down my leg and arm, which, in my innocence, made me feel warm and special.

The woman beckoned us through the side door of the building, which she then locked behind us. It was very dark, but I was conscious of the familiar smell of the canes stacked up around the large empty room as we walked through. This room was usually a hive of activity as people made their baskets and trays, but it was now eerily silent.

I was led to a back room I hadn't been into before, in which I noticed a sink, a stove, a kettle and cups and a shelf on which there was the comforting sight of a packet of biscuits and a bottle of squash. Nestling amongst the various other containers was an ornate glass dish with a fluted edge standing on little glass feet; I remember it looked so pretty with the sun glinting on it. The dish was full of sugar cubes and the woman reached up to offer me one, but I had barely savoured its sweetness when I heard the door slam shut behind me. As I turned around, I saw Ronald sit down on a chair in the far corner of the room with his back to the door.

Not a word was said as I turned back to face the woman, who handed me another sugar cube. I relished the sweet grainy texture on my tongue as she led me to a wooden trestle bench near Ronald. Then, standing directly in front of where I now sat, the woman swiftly lifted her dress, under which she wore no underwear. In panic and confusion, my glance flitted from him to her and back again in search of some sort of explanation as to what was happening, but the answer lay in the twisted line of Ronald's mouth and the cruel look I'd seen before in his eyes as he shouted in his guttural tones, 'At once, at once!'

I wanted to run, but fear left me frozen as his gangling frame blocked my path to the only exit. Warm tears welled up behind my eyelids as the woman grabbed hold of my head and pulled me roughly between her legs, holding me there in her grip. I can still recall the acrid smell, the sense of breathlessness and, above all, the feeling of helplessness. I didn't put up a fight, as I knew I wasn't strong enough. All I could do was try to block out the reality of my ordeal as the two of them repeatedly touched me and made me touch them in return. When it was finally over, I struggled to put my clothes back on, my trembling fingers fumbling with the buttons of my pretty powder-blue coat. The woman then produced an Easter egg, which Ronald ordered me to eat as she repeatedly pushed it towards my mouth. I tried to overcome my nausea, but just a few mouthfuls caused me to vomit down the front of my beautiful new coat. The pair of them laughed – not the happy laugh of adults indulging a child but a strange mirthless cackle – before Ronald pushed me down into my own mess.

I was given a cloth and bucket, and I felt their eyes bore into me as I cleaned up. All the while Ronald was repeating that I was a filthy, evil bitch, but although I heard his words they didn't hurt me any more; the only place I hurt was between my legs where their fingers had been.

I tried not to look at the stain on my lovely new coat as Ronald and I travelled back home. He never looked at me and soon fell asleep, but despite my exhaustion I had to force myself to stay awake, as I had to watch for our stop and wake him when we arrived back in Redbourn. It was nearly teatime when we got back to the prefab where we lived, and my birth-mother Emily had already prepared a meal, but as I made my way into the house, Ronald roughly pushed me into the kitchen to show his wife the state of my coat. He claimed I'd been greedy by eating a whole Easter egg and made myself sick, adding that I should be punished for being so wicked and that it was Emily's duty to beat me, which she duly did with the wet tea towel he handed to her.

As further punishment for my greed, I was sent to bed with no food or drink, but as I lay in bed I soon heard the door open. Suddenly, Ronald grabbed me out of bed, hissing at me that I was evil, I had deserved the beating and I had to learn how to be good and do as I was told. With that, he punched me full in the stomach, knocking the wind out of me, and left me curled up in a tight ball on my bed as he walked out of the room.

Ronald continued to take me on trips to London, and on the next occasion, as he went about his business, he left me alone in the kitchen area where I'd previously been abused. At first I couldn't help but dwell on the events of that day – I could almost smell my own vomit – but as I sat there in silence I gradually managed to push all thoughts of it further into the depths of my mind.

Despite the return trips, I didn't see the woman with the strange eyes again for some time; that was until one bitterly cold day later that year. We were in Tottenham Court Road, but Ronald had told me to take him to another place further along the same street, and once again we met her outside. We entered the building, and Ronald weighed heavily on my arm, often banging into me as I was pushed down a long dark corridor, with the woman hurrying us both from behind. I began to feel my pulse pounding in my ears; I knew what was about to happen, yet I had no option but to obey.

Light briefly flooded the dark space at the end of the corridor as the woman opened the door to an adjoining room. After we were ushered inside, the door was shut behind me, and I found myself in a large, white, partly-tiled room with pipes running across the ceiling and down the walls and a line of toilet cubicles on one side with a row of sinks on the other. Almost immediately, Ronald pushed me forwards towards the woman as he stood in the doorway blocking my path in case I tried to run. Once again, not a word was uttered between the two of them, merely some unspoken communication punctuated by the occasional grunts and guttural sounds that only compounded my fear and left me rooted to the spot as if every bone in my body were made of stone. I shook with terror and with the cold as the woman hastily removed my clothing and threw it to one side before pushing me down on my knees in front of her. Once more she lifted her skirt to reveal no knickers and my head was pushed between her legs. This time I started to gag and struggled to get up, but Ronald started shouting, 'At once! At once!' before grabbing my hair and forcing my face forwards. I felt her push herself onto my face in a rocking motion, and then I was flung forwards onto my hands and knees as he forced himself into me from behind. The pain was excruciating. I felt as if I was being ripped in two, but just as I cried out he yanked my hair back, pulling my face upwards. There she stood, watching and smiling before lying on the floor in front of me and my face was pushed yet again between her legs.

Mentally, I started to shut down, to float away, spinning and dancing like I used to see the ladies on the *Black & White Minstrel* television show do on Sunday evenings. It was the only way I'd learnt to block out whatever cruelty I was subjected to, to transport myself back to a happy memory filled with music and the sparkly feathery outfits the women wore. I imagined I could see myself there on stage with them, smiling and dancing.

When they had finished, Ronald threw my clothes at me and ordered me to get dressed, which I did. As we found our way down the corridor and back out onto the street, I felt my knickers were soaked through and with each step I could barely cope with the pain. When we eventually got home, I went straight to the toilet and found that not only was my underwear drenched but I had blood all down the inside of my legs. I was so scared; I thought I must be dying, and I cried so hard as I washed my knickers in the sink, frightened I would be in more trouble if my birth-parents saw them. Yet later that evening, Ronald allowed me to stay up and watch *Coronation Street*, and I didn't receive a beating as I had on the last occasion. It was as if nothing had happened – perhaps it hadn't? I never saw the woman again and we never returned to that building; but despite my survival technique of denial, of course it had happened. This had by no means been the first occasion, and it would not be the last.

I had been brought up to live by the rules that children should be seen and not heard, they should speak only when spoken to and come when they are called. Children should keep their own counsel and never bring shame to their parents' doorstep. They should have respect for their elders and do as they are told without question. And whatever happens within the four walls of the family home, it stays there. These rules, taught to me by my grandmother, were supposed to keep me on the straight and narrow and safe within my world, but in my case they were to be the very rules that would keep my secret shame hidden deep inside me for over 40 years.

According to a 2000 study by Cawson et al., cited on the NSPCC website, 7 per cent of children have experienced serious physical abuse at the hands of their parents or carers during childhood; 1 per cent of children aged under 16 experienced sexual abuse by a parent or carer and a further 3 per cent by another relative during childhood. Eleven per cent of children experienced sexual abuse by people known but unrelated to them; 5 per cent of children experienced sexual abuse by an adult stranger or someone they had just met. These figures could be considerably higher; the truth is that no one knows the full extent of sexual abuse, as many people never come forward. And for so many, the effects of abuse may only become apparent much later on, in forms ranging from drug, alcohol, physical and emotional abuse to prostitution, self-harming, eating disorders and depression. It is common for people who have been abused to have problems forming relationships with others, as they often feel unworthy of love. Others will appear to live normal lives, but the truth is that you can never escape the effects of what has been done to you, and the inner silent suffering can send people into a seemingly never-ending downward spiral. They feel like outsiders written off by society, and it affects not only their personal health and well-being but also stretches out to haunt those around them. I have met survivors, some in their 80s, who have suffered this silent shame throughout their lives, believing it to be theirs to carry alone. This is why I firmly believe the cycle must be broken, so that people no longer have to live with someone else's shame whilst others feed off it. It is no longer possible to deny that the evil of abuse exists in our world, hiding behind the most respected of doors and venturing down to the lowest levels of society. As children, we have no control over our bodies, but as adults, we have control over both our bodies and our minds; we can change the way we see the past and the way we wish to see the future. Although we must be responsible for our actions in life, we are not responsible for the hand we are dealt.

All we can do is our best; we cannot carry the shame of other people on our shoulders. I have come to learn you cannot point the finger of blame or hold on to the pain inside of you; you must let it go or it will destroy you as surely as any abuse can.

ONE

Wednesday's Child

Standing before the mirror in her white dress and wedding veil, Emily looked every inch the beautiful blushing bride as her older sister Alice, who had not only made the wedding dress but all the bridesmaids' and pageboys' outfits as well, put the finishing touches to Emily's gown and make-up. A shaft of summer sunlight added further lustre to the glossy raven ringlets of Emily's hair, but she was far too pensive to admire her reflection, her normally full red lips remaining pinched while her once flashing emerald eyes looked dull and distant. Sensing her sister's unease, Alice gently laid a reassuring hand on Emily's arm, but nothing could soothe the bride's sense of impending dread at walking up the aisle of the local village church that day to become Mrs Ronald Baird. This match, however, was her mother Gerti's wish and, as her brother Harry and sisters Lily, Alice and Grace knew all too well, where the family was concerned, their mother's word was law.

The youngest of the five children, Emily had been

born in the spring of 1922 in the front room of the three-up three-down terraced house on the outskirts of Littlehampton, a small family home already bursting at the seams. Her father, Dick, a coach driver, spent long hours working on the round trips from Littlehampton to London. With no laws then to govern the amount of hours a driver could do in one day, Granddad would often drive until he was ready to drop and then grab a few hours' grateful sleep, if he was lucky, before setting off again.

As the driving job was seasonal, my grandparents would often open up their already cramped home to tourists and lodgers to help supplement their income. The children all slept in one room, their parents in another, whilst the third and largest room was reserved for the paying guests. Downstairs was similarly divided, with the central room next to the small scullery serving as the family's living room and kitchen, while the front parlour was the preserve of the lodgers. Life was hard and money remained a constant concern, as it did for most people in those days, but they were by and large a happy family who enjoyed simple pleasures such as walks through the surrounding fields, which stretched as far as the eye could see, visits to the beach nearby and to the local bandstand, where on a Sunday local ladies and gentlemen danced to the music and ate their picnic teas on the grass.

But my mother's family harboured an unspoken secret. My grandmother, Gerti, had performed a home abortion prior to conceiving her youngest child, and on discovering she had fallen pregnant yet again, Gerti tried to abort using a crochet hook, but this time to no avail. Such actions might seem harsh in this day and age, but Gerti was one of eight children herself, and after being orphaned at the age of ten, she had formed a pragmatic iron will while growing up in the poverty of a north London workhouse. Whether her actions had any effect on her unborn child will never be known; however, it quickly became apparent that Emily had been born profoundly deaf.

In those days, many deaf children would have been sent away to an institution, but my grandmother steadfastly refused to let this happen – perhaps she felt some guilt over her baby's disability or perhaps she was simply in denial of it. Instead, she raised her daughter within the family home, and her three other girls took turns to nurse and look after their youngest sister. Despite her seemingly austere nature, Gerti doted on the young Emily, teaching her how to sew, knit, cook and clean, all to the high standards Gerti demanded. My grandmother was also determined to teach Emily how to talk, holding up items or pointing to objects and then making Emily painstakingly repeat the right words until her pronunciation was perfect. During these lengthy lessons, Gerti would also gently place her daughter's fingers to her throat and mouth and then back to her own, so she could copy the vibration and mouth-shape each word made for herself.

When Emily was ten, her parents tried to teach her how to read, using books for children half her age, but this time they did not enjoy quite the same success. Emily would become extremely frustrated and refuse to cooperate, hurling the books to the floor in disgust as she stormed out of the room screaming she was not a baby. For despite the close bond Emily had with her family, especially her sister Alice and her father, a placid, humorous man so different in nature from his wife, Emily's world was often a confusing one, haunted by a peculiar loneliness brought on by its perpetual silence. Even as she grew older, her sisters would have to take turns at night to sit with her until she fell asleep, with Emily clinging tightly to their clothes to make sure they didn't leave her. Each sister would pray she would fall asleep quickly, but as soon as they made to get up from the bed, Emily would waken with tears streaming down her cheeks, pleading with them to stay. When she eventually did fall fast asleep, the patient sister was free to resume the chores she had to finish before it was her time to retire for the night.

Emily's world was further confused at the age of 13, when a place was found for her at a local school. The school had no facilities to deal with a deaf child and, due to her frustration and fear of the unfamiliar surroundings, she soon became so disruptive that the exasperated staff had no other option but to inform her parents they could not keep her. From there, Emily was sent to a convent, as in those days nuns or monks would often educate deaf children. But, once again, they could not cope with her behaviour, and it was not long before Emily was sent home. In desperation, Gerti decided the family should move back to her old neighbourhood in north London, as perhaps it would be easier to find a more suitable establishment there at which Emily could continue her fragmented education. And as fortune would have it, a more illustrious member of the extended family stepped in at this point and not only managed to find Emily a place at a private boarding school for the deaf but also made a sizeable contribution towards her tuition fees.

The specialist school certainly succeeded where the others had failed. It offered Emily a degree of stability, and she remained there happily for the next two years, until she was sixteen years old. But whilst Emily had achieved some stability in her life, the world at large was growing ever more unsettled as the dark clouds of the Second World War loomed ominously above and, prior to the mass evacuations that would soon become commonplace from major cities such as London, the family moved once more to the relative safety of the small village of Redbourn in the Hertfordshire countryside.

Emily had by now blossomed into a beautiful young woman, her striking features, tall slim figure and effortless grace turning many a young man's head as she ambled along the country lanes. But perhaps her most alluring aspect was a happy-go-lucky nature and newfound zest for life; she exuded a youthful self-confidence that was no doubt the result of the tranquillity her new life afforded her after the relative chaos of the previous few years.

As her elder siblings married and left home to start families of their own – with the exception of Alice and her husband Jack, who stayed at home with Gerti – Emily took comfort in the two jobs she'd been able to secure within easy travelling distance of the village, working within the packing departments of two different factories. For despite Emily's natural beauty and charming manner, her mother Gerti was under no illusions as to her deaf daughter's chances in the marriage stakes, nor indeed was Emily herself. With the passing of her father in 1946, mother and daughter were left to grow older together in what had once been a family home bustling with activity.

Emily's time, however, was not divided wholly between work and home, as she had begun to attend a deaf club, a place where she could meet socially with those facing the same difficulties and discuss their experiences. In early 1954, a tall, dark newcomer joined the group, and his attention was immediately drawn to the striking-looking woman in her early 30s. This man was Ronald Baird, her husband-to-be and my birth-father. He asked the resident social worker at the group for an introduction and, sensing a potential relationship, she was only too keen to oblige.

Ronald, who had an older brother called Richard and a younger brother Patrick, had been born and raised in Lincolnshire in a deeply religious family. His father was a vicar, as were five generations of the male line before him, but Ronald's health issues, namely his profound deafness, tunnel vision and ear disorder, had precluded him from following in the family tradition of entering the Church, and the bitter resentment Ronald felt at life's injustices was indelibly etched into his very being. He had been sent away to a conventional boarding school at the age of four, where it was hoped his elder brother would be able to look after him, for, as with Emily's education, no provisions were made for his deafness. Instead, Ronald became not only a natural target for his peers but was also subjected to similar cruelties and rudeness by the teaching staff. It all served to add yet another layer to the silent bitterness with which he shrouded himself.

Due to his apparent dependency, Ronald remained at home well into his 20s, but then two dramatic incidents, which I heard about from other relatives, led to him having to fend for himself. Deaf as he was, Ronald would not have heard the persistent hum of his father's car coming from the garage, but he had seen his father go in there some time before. When his father didn't emerge, Ronald tried to open the garage doors but found them locked from the inside. Ronald knew for certain his father was inside, but he simply turned away and told no one. It was much later before his father's body was discovered slumped in the front seat, poisoned by the carbon monoxide still pumping into the car through the hose his suicidal father had connected to the car's exhaust.

His mother's death was as dramatic as it was untimely. During an argument between Ronald and his brother Patrick, their mother tried to intervene but was accidentally pushed, hitting her head on the brass fender that surrounded the fireplace as she fell. She died instantly, with each sibling vehemently blaming the other for their mother's demise. It led to a rift that neither would ever try to heal.

My knowledge of my birth-father's life from this point up until he met Emily remains sketchy at best; the little I've gleaned is that at some point he became a basket-maker for the Institute for the Blind in London. At that time he was living with two old ladies who rented him a room in their home, but he was eventually asked to leave for 'causing too much trouble'. Soon after this, he first crossed paths with Emily at the local deaf club, and I can only assume he possessed qualities that appealed to her, as she persuaded my grandmother to allow him to stay at their house until lodgings were found for him with a local widow in Redbourn. This lady was in need of the extra income as she had a young disabled daughter and was living off a small pension. But despite her circumstances, she, too, soon sent Ronald from her home, though the reasons were never revealed to Emily or her mother.

He may have had many personal problems, but this did not deter Ronald in his swift pursuit of Emily's hand, and he proposed to her within weeks of their first meeting in 1954. Perhaps Emily saw this as her sole opportunity to emulate her brother's and sisters' happy marriages, and Ronald might have felt the same way. Both were by then 32 years of age, and this seemed the ideal opportunity for them to take their places in normal society, something so long denied to them by their disabilities. Whatever their personal reasons may have been, the marriage was set for June that year. However, Emily's siblings were far from impressed by her fiancé, as they instinctively knew that married bliss and 'happily ever after' were not what Ronald Baird was offering. Always protective towards their youngest sister, they made their feelings known to her as gently as they could, unaware that Emily already had reservations of her own that dated back to the day of the engagement. When she protested that the small diamond ring her suitor offered her must have been extremely expensive, Ronald dismissed her worries by telling her he had bought it for a previous girlfriend some time ago. When the relationship had broken down, he had demanded his ring back. This rang alarm bells for Emily, but she felt caught in a situation already spiralling out of control, for when she mentioned her concerns to her mother, Gerti would have none of it. Surely, she said, Emily could see these were just pre-wedding nerves and everything would be absolutely fine after the big day.

I can only speculate as to which sides of Ronald's nature Emily had already been exposed to that would lead her to plead with her mother on the day itself not to make her go through with the wedding, but her pleas were swiftly silenced. Gerti always had her way, and she was not about to see her last child spurn her one opportunity for a settled married life.

Had Emily's siblings known of the conversation that day, they might have fought their mother on Emily's behalf. They were not given the opportunity, however, and as soon as the pair returned from their honeymoon it became apparent to all that something was desperately wrong. Emily had already become withdrawn and uncommunicative. If asked a question, she would immediately reply, 'Ask my husband', and though she still worked, she rarely went anywhere without Ronald. The carefree laughter she had become known for had been silenced for good.

The couple moved out to live in a rented room quite some distance away in Luton and, separated from her family, Emily was truly in Ronald's clutches. He wasted no time in exerting his control over his wife, refusing to let her use electricity either to cook or see by, and woe betide her if she tried to light the room's small fire for warmth. Instead, they lived off cold meals, read by candlelight and shivered through the long winter's bleak chill. Emily secretly confided in her sister and closest friend, Alice, about the conditions she was being subjected to, and Alice would meet her sister's bus on the Luton Road every day to hand her a flask of soup just so she could have something warm inside her while she was at work. However, it was during a family get-together at my grandmother's house that Ronald's true colours were revealed. As was her way, Gerti rather abruptly told Emily to stand up straight and stop slouching, a typical statement she had made many times before. In an instant, Ronald turned around and punched his mother-in-law full in the face, knocking her to the floor. At that precise moment, my uncle Jack walked into the room, and this normally placid man was so incensed by the outrage he witnessed that he lunged straight for Ronald, grabbing him roughly and warning him he had better not lay a finger on another woman ever again or he would beat him senseless. Confronted by an adversary more threatening than a little old lady, Ronald slumped to the floor, begging my uncle not to hit him before seeming to faint. My auntie Grace had been standing at the sink washing up, and she soon brought the prone Ronald around by pouring a ladle full of dirty water over his face. The whole scene might have been quite comical if my grandmother had not suffered such a sore lip. Ronald quickly learnt from his mistake, as in future all his acts of cruelty and violence took place behind closed doors.

In spite of this altercation, my extended family were

thrilled when Ronald and Emily announced less than a year after their marriage that they were expecting their first child. My grandmother graciously invited the couple back to the family home in Redbourn and made up a bedsit for them in the dining room, while Uncle Jack and Aunt Alice, who by now had their own five-year-old son, Robert, buzzed with excitement and made all the preparations for my impending arrival. It was probably just as well, as my birth-parents showed a surprising lack of interest in the matter.

Emily sailed through the pregnancy without any complications, and on a bitterly cold February night the household was woken in the early hours by her crying out. I was on my way. Uncle Jack hastily threw on his clothes over the top of his pyjamas and raced off at top speed through the icy night to the nearest phone box. An ambulance took Emily to hospital alone, as, for whatever reason, Ronald chose not to go with her. It must have been absolutely terrifying for her, trapped in her silent world with no one to communicate with and no one to explain what was happening and calm her fears.

On 23 February 1956, I entered the world, but there was no welcome from proud parents filled with joy, hope and dreams of the future for their first-born. I didn't even enjoy the comfort of my mother's arms, as Emily had been so traumatised by what must have been a difficult birth that she could not bear to have anything to do with me. When the time came for mother and daughter to leave the hospital, my birth-father was noticeable by his absence, and my aunt and uncle came to collect us. Emily still refused to hold me, so, looking deeply into my aunt's eyes, the ward sister gently placed me in her arms and whispered, 'Please take care of her.'

We returned to the family home, and for my birth-parents life continued pretty much as if nothing had happened. It was only after a great deal of persuasion that Emily would take any part in my daytime feeds, and her most active role in looking after my day-to-day needs was to occasionally dress me and rock me in the manner of a child playing with a doll. Little was known about post-natal depression at the time, and she may very well have been suffering from this, but the bond between mother and daughter was non-existent. Meanwhile, my birth-father's interest was confined to putting on a show for any visitors to the house, at which point I instantly became 'his little girl'. At all other times, I remained invisible to them both. It was not unusual for them to go out of the house, sometimes for hours on end, without even telling anyone that they had left me alone in my cot. On one of these occasions, I was heard screaming at the top of my lungs because the cot blanket had started to smother me and I'd woken up in a panic. As ever, Aunt Alice came to the rescue, as it was she who looked after me as well as looking after my grandmother and acting as surrogate mother and childminder to any of my many cousins who might be staying over at the house.

Three weeks after my birth, the local council offered my birth-parents their own accommodation in a prefab about a mile away from the family home. They eagerly accepted the offer and packed their belongings for the move. There was one 'possession', however, they had no intention of taking with them. Without any attempts to ask for help or discussions as to why they couldn't cope with a newborn child, Emily and Ronald literally left my aunt and uncle holding the baby. 'You have her,' they said, 'we can't be bothered. You have her.' And with that, I was left behind.

TWO

Calm Before the Storm

With my birth-parents gone, my grandmother's house on Shepherds Lane became a child's paradise, and my earliest memories are for the most part filled with love and laughter. Auntie Alice and Uncle Jack loved me as they would their own daughter, and from the moment I learnt how to speak I referred to them as Mum and Dad, having little or no memory of Emily or Ronald. Their son Robert, who was five years older than me, was my brother, and we played and fought like all siblings do.

The house itself was a little chalet bungalow positioned at the end of a quiet road, and the low garden wall struggled to hold the mass of rose bushes my grandmother had planted there over the years. On long lazy summer days, the air was filled with the sweet heady scent of flowers and the continual drone of busy bees. The large dark-green front door had a brick porch over it with a small open-arched window to one side, and this often doubled up as a very good 'shop' or 'stationmaster's' window, depending on what game we children were playing on any given day. Inside, the front room of the house was the dining room, which was used for special occasions such as Christmas, but mostly it doubled up as an extra bedroom for guests.

Outside at the back, a path led from the kitchen door to the garden beyond, with a high fence dividing us from our neighbours. To the back of the house stood the lean-to porch and, as we children were outside more than we were in, many happy afternoons were spent playing under the lean-to as the rain showered down around us. At the end of the side alley towards the front of the garden was the old air-raid shelter Uncle Harry had built during the war, which had now become part of our kids' playground. We were told we weren't allowed to play inside it because it went underground, but this only added to its mystery, and we let our imaginations run wild as to what lay behind the barricaded door. Often we'd try to scare each other with stories of how there were still German soldiers hiding down there, but our tales can't have been too frightening as the large sunken area in front of the door had been filled with sand, and many a sand 'cake' or 'pie' was made there, decorated with flowers plucked from an overhanging bush. The gentle slope of the shelter's roof made it ideal for little arms and legs to scamper up, and from its summit we could survey our entire world. The descent, however, was a far from dignified one, as we slid down on our bottoms, and the thick white knickers I wore, as was the fashion for children in those days, would be stretched out of shape. Needless to say, this earned me the nickname 'Droopy Drawers' from my dad and cousins, whilst Mum seemed to be forever good-naturedly sewing up the holes caused by the wear and tear of my games.

A long straight path divided the garden, with the area nearest the house laid to grass and the other section living proof of my grandmother's passion for gardening. Shrubs and flowers of all kinds fought for space and were continually added to, as Gran thought nothing of slipping cuttings into her bag wherever she went. These were then potted up in the greenhouse until they were big enough to plant out. The greenhouse itself, with its large water butt at the top end, stood part-way down the garden. During the summer months, the greenhouse was full to overflowing with ripe tomatoes, and Dad showed me how to nip the ends out of them — a job I quickly grew to love. After washing my hair, I'd make my way to the greenhouse so it would dry quickly in the heat, but the main reason was that I simply loved being surrounded by the heady aroma of ripe tomatoes. Smell is perhaps the most evocative sense in terms of prompting memory, and to this day I adore the scent of tomatoes, as it transports me in an instant to a time of happy innocence.

Just on from the greenhouse was an area reserved especially for the children to indulge whatever interest they had in gardening. By the time I was old enough to take an interest, none of my cousins were keen, so I had the area to myself. Year after year, I cultivated my favourites — marigolds — carefully nurturing each crop and watering them myself from the water butt. And nothing delighted me more than picking them by the armful for any visitors to take away with them. Past my little garden lay the vegetable patch, where Dad grew everything and anything to help feed the family, and in summer we were blessed with all sorts of fresh soft fruits just ripe for the plucking. A giant rhubarb patch at the end marked the start of the spinney, and the leaves were so large that we children delighted in the fact we could shelter under them and not be seen. On occasions we'd sneak a handful of sugar from the kitchen and feast on rhubarb stalks underneath the leaves until gluttony would force one and all on a hurried trip to the toilet! Amongst the trees was one huge Victoria plum, and Robert and I would occasionally be caught by Mum, lying on its long low branches with plum juice all over our mouths.

Even when the long hot summer days gave way to an autumnal chill, our home still lost none of its appeal. Bonfire nights were a particularly special occasion, as all of the extended family, with the exception of Emily and Ronald, gathered together. With Mum and Dad's help, we children began making the Guy weeks beforehand and, once finished, he would sit in a chair under the lean-to so that we could admire our handiwork before the big night itself. Dad's preparation began even earlier, as all through the year he saved suitable branches for the bonfire and collected boxes that would be stuffed with paper at the very last moment, to save them from being drenched in a rain shower and ensure they were bone dry for the fire.

As darkness fell on Bonfire Night, the expectation was palpable. My aunts and uncles would arrive with more fireworks to add to the supply Dad had already bought, while Mum busied herself in the kitchen, preparing jacket potatoes wrapped in foil and flasks of hot soup as thick juicy sausages sizzled away in the oven. Dad always bought a big bag of chestnuts to add to this delicious feast, which were also wrapped in foil, and once the flames of the bonfire had truly taken hold, the chestnuts and potatoes would be placed around the lapping flames, wafting out a tantalising aroma that made our mouths water.

With hurricane lamps hung from the trees to illuminate the spectacle, the 'oohs' and 'ahs' of children and adults alike rose through the branches as each firework thrilled us, our fingers burning on the hot potatoes and sweet-smelling chestnuts. Tired and very smoky from the evening's display, we would trudge back to the house for a hot bath in front of the kitchen fire as Dad and my grandmother put their feet up. Bath-times were an extension of the fun, as we would all sing at the tops of our voices, everything from nursery rhymes to favourites from West End musicals and other popular songs of the day. Shepherds Lane was often filled with the happy sound of children's singing voices, as my cousins Heather and Peter had a portable record player and we would sing and dance for hours to favourites such as 'Bachelor Boy' and 'Little White Bull'. When I was alone, I would even dress up the Hoover and pretend it was my partner as I danced to the music in front of the big mirror in the hallway. I so loved my home and the games we all played.

It seemed the only real cloud that hung over my childhood was the confusion caused on the rare occasions my birth-parents came to call. Those were the only times gloom seeped into the house, and I would be frightened by Ronald banging and shouting about things I simply didn't understand. No one ever tried to hide from me the fact that Emily and Ronald were my 'parents', but this word made no impression on me. After all, I already had a mother, father and brother, didn't I? Perhaps the only time I questioned this myself was when I went along to my brother Robert's school sports day when I was about three years old. I was so proud of him as I watched him compete. I too was entered into an under-fives race, which I won, and at the end of the afternoon I had to go up to the awards table to collect my prize. As I stood there beaming, I was asked what my name was and I replied Isobel Baird. I was then asked if I had any brothers or sisters at the school, and I told them, 'Yes, Robert Langley's my brother,' only for everyone to burst out laughing. I remember my mum looking so awfully embarrassed, and I couldn't help but burst into tears, thinking I had somehow upset Mum and brought shame on myself. It was the first time in my life I was made to feel different from everyone else, but it wouldn't be the last, and I have never forgotten that feeling.

There were times when my birth-parents insisted that I go home with them for a visit and, according to my mum, I would always return very sad and withdrawn. When I was about two and a half, Ronald wanted to take me to stay with his old aunt Ethel in the West Country, and I can still vividly recall the smell of burning coal that filled the station, the engines hissing steam and the ominous clunk of the dark-green carriage doors as they were slammed shut. Ronald held me up to the carriage window just before we departed, and as I peered through the glass I could make out my mum and dad waving to me from the platform. In an instant, I realised that these two strange people I could not understand, who shouted and made strange noises, were taking me away from the security of the parents I loved. In my all-consuming panic, I reached out my arms and screamed for Mum to take me back, and I could see the tears streaming down her face as she mouthed for me to be a good girl. As the train slowly lurched forward, I could see Dad lead Mum away from the platform to their car, and my screams were drowned out by the whistle's shrill blow. Within two days, my mum received a telegram from Great Aunt Ethel pleading with her to come and collect me, as she could not cope with both my birth-parents and a distraught little girl who kept crying for her mum. Uncle Harry drove Mum down to pick us up, and even sitting on the back seat in the safety of my mum's arms I was still terribly upset. Perhaps it was this ordeal that led to me being terribly sick down the front of Mum's yellow-and-white checked dress with its scooped neckline. My vomit sat in her bra and all she could do was stuff hankies down her front in a vain attempt to soak it up and mask the dreadful smell.

Our own family holidays may have been modest by today's standards, but they were very happy affairs. We had an old white RAF bell tent in which we'd go camping, and the car would be loaded to bursting point as we kids were squeezed inside. We would usually set off in the small hours and stop on the roadside for breakfast, which was a treat in itself.

During the holidays, we would play on the beach for hours on end and eat outdoors with the sound of seagulls above and the briny smell of the sea whetting our appetites as we crunched our way through sand-filled sandwiches. If the weather turned, we simply sat cocooned in the car, cracking crabs' legs from the bag we shared and picking out the meat as the rain bounced a tattoo on the roof. They were such happy times, and I thought they would never end. I had no idea of just how fragile my carefree existence had been and that it was about to change for ever.

One afternoon I sat on the floor happily playing with the small second-hand toy piano Dad had bought for me. I loved my piano, with its shiny red paintwork, and was so absorbed in my game that I didn't realise that my birth-parents had arrived at the house on one of their rare visits. I had just returned from a friend's birthday party, and Mum asked me to fetch the cake I'd brought home and show it to Ronald. I didn't hear when or how the argument started, but as I returned to the living room I saw my birth-father was angry about something and had begun to make his angry guttural shouts. Emily sat subdued in the corner as I approached him warily with the piece of birthday cake in my outstretched hand, hoping this might in some way calm his anger. Instead, with one swift swipe he knocked the cake to the floor, and I stood in shocked silence as he proceeded to stamp my beloved piano to pieces. Mum ordered both Ronald and Emily from the house and, once they'd gone, we sat clinging to each other as I cried, heartbroken over the loss of my piano. It was only many years later that Mum told me Ronald had come that day to demand I was sent back to them permanently when I reached the age of seven. At that point, I would be moving up to the junior school just across the way from my birth-parents' home, and Ronald reasoned that at that age I would be able to look after both of them as well as myself. My birth-father's plan was for me to sell door-to-door the crafted wicker baskets he was now making from home for the Royal Institute for the Blind.

For the next 12 months, Mum and Dad fought desperately with the authorities to keep me with them, but they were repeatedly told that Ronald and Emily were repentant at having abandoned me and that my place was with them. The silent threat was that Mum and Dad could spend all the money they had on legal proceedings but their attempts to keep me would be in vain. Unbeknown to me, my fate was sealed.

THREE

Into His Clutches

A bitterly cold wind whipped through the trees that February evening as Robert and I helped Mum to clear up in the kitchen after tea and waited for Dad to return home from work. The glowing heat from the stove kept us warm as we busied ourselves, and we were all just thankful not to be caught outside in the persistent rain that hammered at the windows. Suddenly, the back door burst open and an icy blast swept through the kitchen. There, filling the doorframe in the half-light, stood Ronald. I had just turned seven years old and, as he'd previously threatened, he had now come to collect what was his. As ever, his face looked pinched and pale, and his twisted lips took on what I would come to recognise as a customary smirk of disgust. Standing 6 ft 4 in. tall yet extremely thin, his black hair parted at the side, he looked for all the world like a taller version of Adolf Hitler but without the moustache.

Mum instinctively took hold of me and tried to usher me from the room, but my birth-father was not to be denied. He lurched towards us and grabbed my arm, roughly pulling me towards him as if I were nothing more than a mere rag doll. There'd been no prior warning of his arrival, so Dad was not there to protect us, and Mum had not had the chance to prepare me for this. We were powerless to resist Ronald, and I was not even allowed to say goodbye once Mum had quickly packed some clothes for me. I was simply whisked out of the front door and into the cold, dark early evening.

I shivered with cold and apprehension as we made our way to the housing estate where Ronald and Emily now lived, and my grandmother's rules replayed over in my mind. Surely the adults who had made this decision knew what was best for me? For the first seven years of my life, I'd never had cause to question Gran's rules, but little did I know they were now about to stop me from being saved or saving myself. I was also about to be subjected to a whole new set of rules.

I was not expecting a warm greeting on arriving at the house and nor did I receive one; instead, I was shown to my bedroom and left there. I was utterly confused and miserable, having no idea why this had happened to me. I eyed my new surroundings for the first time, taking in the details that would become indelibly etched into my mind over the coming years. On first impression, my room was quite pretty, with its pink-and-red rose-patterned wallpaper and golden curtains which, when drawn, gave a warm comforting glow to the room. The room was furnished with a small bed and a chest of drawers, and in the corner, built into the wall, there was a wardrobe with metal doors and shelves. I soon learnt that opening the heavy doors, which had two air vents three-quarters of the way up, made a piercing noise like nails being dragged down a blackboard. In time, this wardrobe would take on the role of hiding place or prison, depending on whether I'd chosen or been forced to be locked away in there. But the initial change I had to grow accustomed to on that first night was sleeping alone for the first time in my life, and in the solitude I so missed my brother Robert.

The following morning, I took in more of my new surroundings and soon found them to be as cold and uninviting as the couple that lived there. The house was a prefab set in a small estate on one side of a large municipal park where children could play. The estate had been built as quickly and as cheaply as possible after the war, and all the houses were identical in shape and size. I soon discovered that it was not only my wardrobe that creaked when its doors were opened: all the metal cupboards and drawers in the kitchen also made that eerie screech; unlike me, however, my profoundly deaf birth-parents were of course immune to these noises. The sitting room had a small fire that even in the middle of winter was rarely lit unless my birth-father gave permission, and a narrow hall led from this room onto two bedrooms and a darkly painted bathroom.

Whereas my grandmother's house could boast the sweet aromas of her rose bushes in the garden or the stash of apples she kept wrapped up in her bedroom, the overriding smell in Ronald and Emily's house was that of mothballs and TCP. There were no carpets or rugs on the floors, and Ronald had sanded down all the wooden furniture so it looked particularly dull and lifeless. The only colour in the entire house was provided by the plastic tulips and daffodils for which Emily had painstakingly collected tokens from packets of washing powder, and she was immensely proud of these fake blooms. The small gardens at the front and back of the house contained no flowers, just a low privet hedge circling the perimeter, and the only feature was the coalhouse near the kitchen door. This, like my wardrobe, served as a hiding place when I needed it, although I had to be very careful not to dirty my clothes on the thick black lumps, as this would be sure to earn me a beating.

The house may have been basic, but it was the fact it was so lifeless compared to my grandmother's home that struck me the most. Any spark had been doused by my birth-father's tyrannical regime: he saw himself as the undisputed head of a household in which both Emily and I were possessions that he could do with as he pleased.

Ronald seemed to run our lives by an invisible clock inside his head. All meals were at set times governed by him, and there could be no delay. If we had toast for breakfast, it was only ever one slice, thinly buttered, and the portions for all of our meals were similarly monitored. Meals were invariably cold slices or food that could be cooked very quickly, and when Emily was permitted to use the stove, woe betide her if she did not cook on a very high heat for the shortest time possible so as not to use up too much gas. Unfortunately, this meant that even cooked meals, which usually consisted of cubed Spam mixed with an Oxo cube and baked beans and topped with instant mashed potato, were either burnt, or cold and raw in the middle. Alternatively, he would suddenly decide on a whim that the most economical method was to cook everything on an extremely low temperature for longer, which only resulted in meals being either hard as a rock or dry as a bone. When we went to the toilet, we were only allowed to use one square of toilet paper per visit, and if the box of paper was used up quicker than he expected it to be, all hell would break loose and either Emily or I would receive a savage beating. Treats and pleasures of any kind were not permitted; he decided when we went to bed, when the lights went out, when we ate, when we had heating and when we opened our bowels. A hard, unemotional man, he never ceased his criticism of either Emily or myself, and he appeared to derive a lot of pleasure from hurting his wife and daughter, as it was the only time he seemed happy. It must have been soul-destroying for Emily, too, as Ronald would not allow her to speak in front of any guests on account of her being, in his words, 'stupid', and on reflection it's no wonder she lost all interest in life.

Emily was a good foot shorter in height than her husband, and her face was kind but perpetually sad. The brief moments of happiness that I can recall in that house were when she tried to teach me how to sew and knit. Emily would secretly buy small bars of chocolate and cut them into tiny squares and, as we sat there working, we'd pop these tiny portions into our mouths, just big enough so we could eat them without actually chewing. Ronald was none the wiser and it remained our little secret, perhaps the only bond ever forged between me and either of my birth-parents.

As I had only had very sporadic contact with Ronald

and Emily, I couldn't understand the harsh, rasping sounds they made, and for a long time their only method of communicating with me was pointing, pushing or shouting incomprehensibly. The only contact between Emily and Ronald seemed to be when he was shouting at her, although it was hard for me to distinguish between normal communication and verbal arguments, as it all sounded the same. The only indication that another row had erupted was when Ronald started flailing his arms around as he used sign language, a form of communication only he was allowed to use in the house, as it was deemed wrong in those days for the deaf to sign; they were encouraged to lip read and use their hands only for spelling instead. Once my birth-father started to express himself in this way, I knew it was only moments before he would begin staggering all over the room, his face bright red as if it would burst as he forced Emily to look at him. She was rather lucky in that way, for if she wanted to ignore his rant, she could simply turn her back. I on the other hand didn't have that luxury and, whatever I had done to cause his latest outburst, it would more often than not end in a beating. I became as confused as I was frightened, and I just couldn't understand how I had suddenly become such a difficult child.

As the weeks passed, I felt even more bewildered by what had happened to me. I missed my family so very much and, however hard I tried, I couldn't understand why I could no longer live with them. Had I done or said something wrong and my punishment was to be sent away? Was I simply not wanted any more?

As I had moved up to the junior school near my

birth-parents' home, it was now my responsibility to get myself there each day, something which was totally alien to me as Mum had always taken me before. But once inside the school gates I felt at ease. School became a haven, as it was the only place that now retained any sense of normality. However, despite my worst fears, I had by no means been abandoned by the family I still regarded as my own. Ronald had banned Mum from seeing me but, as Emily had given up her job when I came to stay with them, Mum was able to visit her sister when I was at school and Ronald was out, to see if I was all right. Emily always assured her that everything was fine, but Mum remained unconvinced and eventually approached the local vicar about her fears over me. She expressed her concerns, explaining that she believed Ronald to be mentally unstable, and begged him to intervene. But the vicar told her in no uncertain terms how very wrong she was and that she should now leave me alone. My birth-father was a good and God-fearing man and, if anything, she was the problem and must stop interfering. Mum also approached social services again but to no avail; they urged her to leave me alone, as Ronald had reassured them there were no problems and that I would settle down in time. In a last-ditch attempt, Mum went to my school and spoke with the headmaster, who was unaware of the details of my altered home life; but all he could report was how settled I appeared, which during the school day I was.

Events were by now gathering pace and would conspire to keep me trapped in Ronald's clutches. My grandmother was now in a nursing home a couple of miles away, and my mum saw an opportunity to spend some precious time with me by suggesting she might take me to see her. Surprisingly, Ronald agreed. As I waited for my first visit from Mum since I'd been taken away, I ached with the hope that she was actually coming to take me home. At the nursing home, it frightened me to see my grandmother lying in a strange bed in a place I didn't recognise, but in just a few short weeks everything in my life had inexplicably changed. I understood none of it, other than that I must continue to be well behaved and do as I was told. It was a phrase even Mum used on the return bus journey as she tried to explain why I could not go back to her, Dad and Robert. I started to cry and begged her to take me back, promising that I'd be a good girl and explaining just how thoroughly miserable I was. There was nothing she could do, however, and I returned to my birth-parents' house with hopes crushed.

A few weeks later, my grandmother passed away and the old family home in Shepherds Lane was to be sold so that the proceeds could be divided between the siblings. By the autumn of 1963, my family had moved to live with Mum's brother and his wife about four miles away, but for me they might just as well have moved to the moon.

On the day of their move, Ronald gave Mum and Dad permission to say goodbye to me. Mum gave me a supply of writing paper and stamped addressed envelopes with which she urged me to keep in touch. She also gave me a photograph of her, myself, Dad and Robert taken in the garden just the summer before. I somehow managed to control the pangs this image gave me, and when Mum told me to be brave and not cry, for the first time I felt no tears welling up despite the constriction in my chest. As I watched Dad's old car drive off with Mum and Robert waving to me through the back window, I felt cold, as if something had died inside me. It was like the last remnants of hope had left me and all that remained was the dark realisation that I would never be able to return to my old life.

As the car turned the corner, I trudged silently back into the house, but no sooner had the front door shut behind me than Ronald lashed out, striking me with such force to the side of the head that I fell back against the hall wall, knocking a vase off a small table that sat there. While I was dazed and sobbing, the pain didn't register immediately; all I was aware of was Ronald ranting in that guttural, almost feral way of his, and I cowered on the floor in sheer terror. He snatched the photograph Mum had given me from the floor, took one glance at it and then proceeded to rip it into tiny pieces, laughing cruelly in my face as he did so. As he confiscated the writing materials I'd been given, I turned to look at Emily, my eyes silently pleading for support and protection, but while I spotted the tears welling up in her own, she simply turned her back on the scene and walked slowly into the living room. Alone now, I screwed my body up into the tightest ball I could, too scared to know what to do, too scared even to move, only the pain which now throbbed in my head acting as confirmation that this bizarre unprovoked attack had taken place. For what seemed like hours, I could hear them both arguing in the living room, the grunts only punctuated by the muffled thud of furniture being thrown or the sound of Emily sobbing.

Night had fallen by the time anyone came back into the hall, where I still lay huddled on the floor. I'd been too scared to go to the bathroom, even though it was only a couple of feet away, and Ronald found me sitting in my own urine. He yanked me from the floor, his strong fingers digging into my arms, all the while his cruel mouth spitting words at me I couldn't decipher. I could smell his rancid breath, a stench I can still remember to this day. After being shoved into the bathroom, I stood silently shaking in the corner as he ran the bath. Suddenly my clothes were wrenched from me, and I was hoisted up then dunked fully into the cold water, its icy bite sending spasms through my body and setting my teeth chattering in my head. I was ordered to stand up and scrub myself, which I dutifully did while he scrutinised me with burning eyes and that cruel twist to his mouth. Afterwards, I was sent to bed without any food or drink, and I shivered in terror under the blankets in case he came back in. I could hear them now moving about and getting ready for bed themselves, but I would not let myself slip into sleep until I was sure he would not return.

The following morning, a Sunday, I was frogmarched to the local church by both of them, where I was to atone for my sins of the previous day. It was the only time they came with me, as I was sent on my own from that Sunday on, but the rest of the day marked out how my time would be spent at the weekends. After returning from the service and being allowed a small lunch, I was marched by Ronald into the living room, where I was ordered to kneel in front of the sofa and a large old Bible was thrust in front of me. I had to maintain the kneeling position at all times, and it was not long before the floor, on which we had no coverings, began cutting into my knees. Ronald kept pointing at the Bible and pushing it in front of me. I finally realised he wanted me to read it and tried to comply, but I barely understood a word on the pages in front of me. However, my attempts seemed to appease him, as at least he stopped shouting. He sat down in his chair by the fire, and while I was conscious of his eyes boring into me I was far too scared to look up. I stayed in that position for what seemed like hours, as Emily joined us and sat silently in the other chair embroidering a tablecloth.

FOUR

The Downward Spiral

By the following year, Ronald's deteriorating eyesight meant he was forced to work making his wicker baskets from home, and with his long-term aim of training me to look after both him and his wife, I was forced into taking an active role. Ronald's day began at seven-thirty in the morning, and he would toil solidly until six in the evening, sitting perched on a wooden base with another smaller board on his legs onto which the basket would be placed whilst he worked. As each layer was woven, he would grunt as he hammered the new section down into place. When each new batch of canes arrived from the institute warehouse, it was my responsibility to sort them into batches according to their height and thickness, tie them up and stack them in the hallway outside my bedroom. Outside the prefab, at the front, stood a large oblong metal tank filled with water, and as each new bundle was needed for Ronald's work, it was my job to prepare them by soaking them in the tank. This would soften the canes and make them more pliable to work with. We didn't have a telephone, so when a certain type of cane was running low, I had to go to the phone box past the local parade of shops and call the suppliers to order the new materials that Ronald needed. I always had to remember to take a box with me to stand on so I could reach the receiver.

These chores in themselves were not unreasonable, but my daily work by no means ended there. My birth-father had produced a folder containing pictures of all the goods he made and the corresponding price list, as well as a piece of typed paper on the first page explaining what other wicker goods he was capable of crafting. Armed with this homemade catalogue and a batch of flyers he'd made himself, I would walk the streets of the local village, knocking on doors trying to sell his wares. If people expressed any sort of interest, I'd try to get them to place an order. I would write these orders down in a separate book and give the customer a duplicate copy. If no one was home, I would hastily scribble a quick note to remind myself which house it was and place a flyer inside the letterbox before returning on another day in the hope of a sale. Most of the people I approached were nice, probably on account of me being the youngest door-to-door salesperson they had ever seen, or they were uninterested. Sometimes the door would be slammed shut in my face, and on a few occasions a more forthright householder would bellow 'fuck off' at me.

I made my rounds in all weathers and would often return home soaked to the skin, shivering with cold or suffering from painful chilblains on my toes after having been caught in yet another downpour. Yet whatever rudeness I encountered, disappointments I faced in trying to make a sale, or discomfort and fatigue I suffered working such long hours, they quickly paled in comparison to the prospect of going back without having sold anything. Just one sale during my travels would probably save me from a beating, but if I dared go home with no orders at all, I knew I faced his heavy blows raining down on me as he grunted what a lazy, wicked girl I was before sending me to bed with no food.

Not only was I now earning my keep, I had also become Emily and Ronald's eyes and ears. Ronald had given me a laborious course of lessons in finger-spelling, and my ability to lip read had improved to the point where I could understand their voices and distinguish different words. Emily also secretly taught me the basics to signing, which I found to be far more fun, but this was always done well away from my birth-father's prying eyes. On the occasions we were caught, a huge argument would ensue during which he would hit us both on the hands and arms as he screamed at us.

In March of 1964, ties to my old life became ever more tenuous when Mum came to visit in order to tell us that the family was moving away to Cambridgeshire. In partnership with Uncle Harry, his wife Ann and her daughter Susan, Mum and Dad were going to buy the local shop and post office in one of the small villages there. On the day after they left, I cycled back to Shepherds Lane and stood outside the house where I'd spent my happy early years. All the familiar features were still there: my grandmother's rose garden to the front, bursting at the seams with scent and colour;

through the windows I could see the garden and the spinney where I had climbed the trees until my arms ached. I could make out the greenhouse and imagined the heady aroma of tomatoes filling my nostrils as my hair dried. But the house was not the same any more; it was no longer my home, just an empty shell now that Mum, Dad and Robert were gone, and I pedalled back to my birth-parents feeling even more of an outsider.

But still I couldn't let go. The house hadn't yet been sold, and Mum's younger sister, Aunt Grace, now lived there with her boyfriend Charlie and her two children Heather and Peter, so whenever I got the chance I'd sneak out on my bike and make my way back there, like some reluctant homing pigeon. On some occasions, I was even given permission to visit, and during the summer months my trips increased, giving me a welcome reprieve from the unhappiness of my day-to-day existence. When Charlie's son Owen came to stay on holiday, I often played in the garden with him. Charlie would join in the games and chase us around the garden until he caught us, when he would tickle me until I squealed. Charlie would also put me on his back and run around the garden with me, his fingers laced under my bottom. When his fingers began slipping into my knickers and touching me down below, I said nothing. I didn't know it was wrong, and it was the only form of attention I'd received since Mum had left.

It was not long before Aunt Grace, Charlie and my cousins moved away and the house of my childhood belonged to strangers, but before all ties with this happy home were cut, Emily began visiting her sister in the evenings, leaving me on my own with Ronald. On one such evening, after tea had been cleared away and I'd done the washing up and put everything back in its proper place, I was sent to get ready for bed. Wearing my nightie and dressing gown, I came back through to the living room and sat on the sofa watching television prior to being sent to bed at half past seven. I could see Emily in the kitchen wearing an ivory dress with large black polka dots on it. She'd draped a cardigan around her shoulders and had her shoes on all ready to go out into the balmy summer's evening. So, considering it was so early and my birth-mother was obviously all set to go out, I was very surprised when Ronald entered the living room wearing his pyjamas and dressing gown. Emily stood in the kitchen door facing the sitting room as Ronald entered from the opposite direction. Not a word was spoken between them, but Emily just kept staring at her husband with a look I couldn't comprehend. Then, with obvious reluctance, she pulled herself away from the room and left the house via the back door.

My glance shifted instinctively to the clock, which it always did around bedtime, as I didn't want to give Ronald any excuse to lose his temper. However, I had always wanted to be allowed to stay up late enough to watch an episode of *Coronation Street* and, as the opening credits rolled, it seemed tonight might just be the night. I made to go to bed, but my birth-father told me to stay. I felt very grown up as I sat enthralled, listening to the characters and the tales they had to tell, but as Ena Sharples stood talking to her friend Minnie Caldwell in the corner shop, I became aware of Ronald shifting himself on the sofa. I turned to look at him and saw his pyjama trousers were now wide open and the white cord hung either side. I stared at his erect penis, not that I truly understood what it was. I had never seen a penis before apart from accidentally catching my brother in the toilet once, and his didn't look like this. I looked up into his face in search of an explanation, but all I saw was his unusually wide bright eyes and the now too-familiar cruel twist to his mouth. Without so much as a word, he grasped my hand and positioned it on himself, forcing me to perform the motion he wanted and holding it there tightly so I could not snatch my hand away. I instinctively knew something wasn't right, and I struggled to free my hand, telling him 'no', only for him to suddenly grab my hair with his free hand and shove my head face-down into his lap. He pulled me back up to face him and barked that I must put it in my mouth before shoving my face back down again. Terrified, I could feel the blood pounding in my ears as I was forced to comply with his demand, and as the wailing theme tune of *Coronation Street* faded into the distance, he repeatedly pushed and pulled my head up and down, faster and faster, until I felt as if I would choke on the hot liquid that now filled my mouth and caused me to gag.

After he'd flung me aside, I slid to the far corner of the sofa while he sat sprawled out opposite me, his head flung back and his eyes shut. It seemed like an eternity that I sat frozen in fear, all the while conscious of his breathing slowly returning to normal. Then suddenly he lunged for me again, the hair pulled to breaking point from my scalp as he hauled me to my feet and dragged me to my room, all the while telling me just how evil I was. Once inside, I expected a beating, but it never came; the door was slammed shut, and I sat in abject confusion as my eyes adjusted to the darkness, unable to fully comprehend what had just happened to me. Sometime later, I heard Emily return, and I silently prayed for her to come in and see me. Instead, she simply made her way to her bedroom without checking on me. But then she never did, as I believe she was as scared of her husband as I was, so why should this night be any different? With the evening's events replaying themselves in my mind, I finally drifted off into my own nightmares.

The next morning, I woke to shafts of sunlight highlighting the roses on the wallpaper. My heart was pounding in my chest, as I didn't know what to expect once I ventured out of my room. Yet on meeting Ronald and Emily, it was as if the previous evening had never happened. I simply got myself ready, had my breakfast and made my way to school, all the while silently dwelling on the fact that he'd hurt me. I knew I hadn't liked what he'd done, but I was unaware that it was wrong or bad. After all, I was only eight years old, and I'd been brought up to respect adults and do as they said without question.

From that day on, I dreaded every moment I was left alone in the house with my birth-father, but he never repeated that evening on the sofa. Ronald would hurt me in many other ways instead, both physically and mentally. He never failed to remind me at every opportunity how evil I was, often telling me that I wouldn't amount to anything and how his brother Patrick's children were so much better than me. He seemed to delight in informing me that, when he died, all of his money would go to them, but the notion of inheritance had little meaning to an eight year old. All his words did was confirm the fact that I was unloved, unwanted and worthless.

He had also taken to bathing me in private, and I would have to stand up in the bath throughout as he soaped and rinsed me down, over and over again. I loathed his touch as I stood there self-consciously, unable to cover myself. If I complained, though, he would hit me as hard as he could, so I soon learnt it was better to keep quiet.

FIVE

Used and Abused

After moving to live with my birth-parents, I soon learnt that if you don't like the world you live in, you have to create your own, and as I increasingly retreated into myself, I let my mind drift back to the happy days at my grandmother's house. Blanking out my current surroundings, I daydreamed of sitting in the Shepherds Lane garden shelling peas or watching Mum picking mint and turning it into her delicious mint sauce. On one occasion, Mum asked me to top and tail the gooseberries for the crumble she was making for our pudding, and I sat contentedly in the sunshine against the lean-to, working away. After a while, Mum came out to collect the gooseberries and was surprised at how few I'd managed to prepare until she realised I'd thought topping and tailing the gooseberries also entailed shaving off all of their hairs! Needless to say, I was good-naturedly teased for ages after that.

At other times I would dream of dressing up in my grandmother's old clothes and hats and dancing in front of the hall mirror as 'Music While You Work' played on the radio, but then I would hear Ronald's gruff voice calling me and I would be dragged sharply back into the harsh reality of my new life. I knew that Ronald believed I was bad and evil, and I thought that if only I could learn to be a good girl then perhaps my birth-parents would love me as my family had.

Increasingly from now on, Emily began to complain of feeling unwell and appeared to suffer from undefined and prolonged illnesses that she claimed left her constantly drained and unable to cope with most of the household chores. For Ronald, the solution was simple, and now on returning from school it became my duty not only to help him with his cane work and the door-to-door sales but also to cook our meals each evening. I did all the local shopping and once a week I had to escort them both to Luton so we could do the larger shop at the supermarket. I was by now able to communicate with them more easily, as I'd become quite proficient at lip reading, so I was useful as their interpreter for the outside world. However, these trips filled me with absolute dread, as to the outside world my birth-parents were an oddity to be ignored or sniggered at from the other side of the street. With each trip, I became increasingly self-conscious and embarrassed by strangers staring at us.

My interpretation skills were also used to relate the news to my birth-parents each evening and, whilst I may not have understood in depth, I was probably better informed than most children my age as I told them about what was going on in the outside world.

Emily had two cats that she appeared to love dearly;

she certainly lavished far more affection and attention on them than she ever did on me. But their welfare also became my responsibility, and it was up to me to clear up their mess, including vomit and diarrhoea, and once I had to dispose of a half-eaten kitten that was found in one of the cats' beds. My regular household chores soon increased to include all the washing and ironing, which was then subjected to Ronald's stringent inspections. It was rarely up to his high standards, though these had not been explained to me, and this would result in a string of his sour-breathed verbal taunts. More often than not, I would be sent to my room, deprived of food and water, and left to pray that Emily might, as she sometimes did, smuggle me in a small piece of chocolate to ease my hunger pains when Ronald wasn't looking. I also made sure to drink heavily from the tap each time I sneaked into the toilet.

Nobody had any idea of what went on within the four walls of that house. On the rare occasions that we had visitors or if we bumped into neighbours out in public, all they would have seen was a well-behaved, extremely quiet little girl. On such occasions, Ronald couldn't sing my praises highly enough, and I became the marvellous child who worked so hard caring for her poor unfortunate parents, but the charade would end the moment that the front door closed.

Ronald now insisted that Emily take a more active role in punishing me, and if he felt she had not been sufficiently severe, he would march me to my bedroom and punch me full in the stomach. This had become his favourite place to hit me, and as I lay almost lifeless and gasping for breath, he would stand over me, admiring his handiwork. Afterwards, he would bundle me into my wardrobe and leave me locked in there for hours on end. On the occasions he was out of sight and I had done something wrong that Emily threatened to tell him about, I would hide in the wardrobe myself, burrowing under the clothes. Then I would peek out through the vents in the doors, dreading the sound of his footsteps in the hall, the sunlight in the room seeming so far away from my dark confinement, where I sat with tears streaming down my face until there were none left to shed.

I learnt pretty quickly, however, that tears were futile, as not only would they result in further punishments but also no one who might help me could hear me cry anyway. I was just a frightened little girl with no voice and a birth-mother too frightened or too uninterested to save her only daughter.

Nightmares now plagued my sleeping hours, and the one I still remember vividly was that of Japanese soldiers armed with guns outside our house intent on killing us as I struggled to rouse Ronald and Emily and lead them to safety. I would shout at them as they lay asleep in bed, but my cries couldn't break through their deafness, and panic would rise in me to the point of hysteria as I heard the soldiers' voices and saw their dark shadows flitting past the windows. I would wake with a start, drenched in sweat and terrified, but I knew better than to hope someone would come to soothe away my fears.

I was already being taken out of school to attend doctors' appointments with Ronald as well as taking him up to London to the eye hospital, and as Emily's mystery illnesses continued, which with hindsight might have been brought on by Ronald's demands that she punish me, I similarly skipped many classes in order to accompany her to the surgery. As a result, I was finding it harder and harder to keep up at school, and once other children become aware of someone 'different' from themselves, they can often pounce on their prey. I desperately wanted to be one of the girls everyone liked, the popular pupils who shared secrets with each other and whose parents greeted them with a hug at the school gates at the end of the day, but instead I had no friends and suffered a silent loneliness. I didn't know why or how, I just knew I was different from them, and so did they. It was only a matter of time before my classmates banded together to pick on me, the outcast. At first it was just name calling — 'Dummies' Kid' or 'Spastics' Kid' would be hissed at me with venom — but soon the insults were accompanied by pushes and kicks, pinches and punches, and the only time I felt truly safe was in the classroom. The teacher's presence meant the other children did not have the opportunity to pick on me, but it was only ever a temporary reprieve.

If I had been fortunate enough to make any friends, I would certainly never have been allowed to invite them home. On my ninth birthday, however, this rule was temporarily relaxed, and I was told I'd be allowed to have a party. I invited as many girls as I could from my class, and on the day itself, I waited anxiously for them to arrive. As the minutes dragged past, however, it was clear that they weren't going to turn up, and by the end of the afternoon, only two girls had arrived. The next day in school, I could see the other girls laughing and talking behind their hands and, after hearing the words 'Dummies' Kid', I knew they were laughing at me. I never asked for another party again.

There were, however, three girls who would sometimes play with me – all of them outcasts like me, so I suppose we must all have been a bit strange in some way. We would sneak away from the others down the alleyway that led to the school gates, and there, using bent pieces of hedging, we amused ourselves in the early autumnal mornings trying to hook spiders' cobwebs that glistened with dew. There was also the bar to the railings on the footpath over which we'd turn and turn again until we fell to the ground dizzy with laughter. There was no opportunity or spare time after school to play with these friends, though, as not only had I become my birth-parents' home help and interpreter but to all intents and purposes I was also a child serf at their beck and call whenever I wasn't in school. And my birth-father still had other 'duties' in store for me.

One night, soon after I'd turned nine years old, I woke to realise that someone had climbed into bed with me. It was my birth-father, and his hands were already all over me. I was scared and confused, as I suspected something like the previous incident on the settee was about to take place.

Nothing could possibly have prepared me for the excruciating pain that burnt through me to the core that night as he anally penetrated my child's body for the first time. Once he'd left the room, I curled myself into a ball beneath the sodden sheets and rocked myself, sobbing into my pillow. The following morning, I was in so much pain that he decided I should be kept off school, and I remained at home for the rest of the week. During that time, he never came near me other than to tell me I was suffering because I was evil. He told me it was all my fault, that I'd brought it on myself, and then forced me to sit and read the Bible before asking God for His forgiveness. I did indeed pray to God: I promised I would always be a good girl and try to make Ronald happy so that he would never feel the need to punish me in this way again, and I also asked Him to bring my Mum and Dad back. God, it seemed, chose to ignore my pleas on both counts.

Once I'd recovered from the physical effects of that first rape, his visits to my room became a regular occurrence, initially about twice a week, but before long I suffered my birth-father's assaults on a nightly basis. Getting ready for bed now held its own fears, as I knew what was coming next and knew that I was powerless to stop it. I would lie in bed willing myself to fall asleep, as just maybe he might then leave me alone, but sleep was impossible and I turned to stone each night as I heard the door open, knowing his rough hands would soon be groping my body. It seemed that my birth-father took great delight in watching my terrified face when he came into my room to hurt me, for no matter how dark the night might be, the street lamp right outside my window always illuminated my room well enough for me to be able to make out the twisted pleasure etched into the features of his face as he stood over me. Sometimes, once he'd finished with me, I would be ordered to stand naked in the middle of the room, silently sobbing in agony as he stared at me with that crooked line to his mouth. He would repeat over and over again that I was wicked and evil, that I would surely go to hell, and this was the reason he had to keep on punishing me in this way.

At times like these, I mentally retreated so far into myself that it was almost as if he wasn't really there, but there was no disguising the physical pain I often suffered down below, and the following morning Emily would get the next-door neighbour to contact the doctor, who would call in to see me after morning surgery. I had to tell him that I was suffering from a stomach ache, and Ronald always stood in the room watching me like a hawk as the doctor examined me. I would have to interpret everything Ronald said for the doctor and his reply in return. Ronald's gaze would stay firmly fixed on my mouth throughout to make sure I did not say anything other than what he wanted me to. Afterwards, as I lay in bed, Emily would come and sit with me. Nothing was said, and there were few soothing words from her, but we would do puzzles on a tray on the bed. In my confused state, it seemed as if these moments of closeness with my birth-mother, the only signs of affection she showed me, were my reward for enduring Ronald's night-time visits.

The repeated rapes did not seem to satisfy my birth-father's lust for cruelty, and soon the dreaded bath times began to occur almost every day immediately after I returned from school. Emily was ordered to stay outside as he rubbed a block of soap hard into a large scrubbing brush whilst I stood naked in the bath. He would then scrub me harshly between my legs, watching my face all the while and ordering me to be quiet. I never made a sound, for I knew no one would hear me if I did, so with all the willpower I could muster I tried to take my mind to another place while I suffered yet another assault at the hands of this man. I later learnt that Mum was aware of Ronald bathing me but not the manner in which he did it. Emily had told her on one of her rare visits to Mum, on which I was never allowed to accompany her, and Mum told her it was wrong and that Emily should be the one to wash me at that age. Emily answered, as she always did, that she was not well enough and said it was now Ronald's job. Mum actually complained to the social services about this, but they certainly took no action that I was aware of, and Ronald continued to bath me up until I was nearly 11 years old.

To help ensure my cooperation and silence, Ronald used promises as well as threats, and he took great delight in telling me that if I did as he said, he would let me see my mum or let me write to her. He must have known I'd never truly given up all hope that things would somehow change, that Mum and Dad would come back to collect me so everything could be as it used to be. However, unlike his threats, his promises were idle, and I never did get to see my mum or write her a letter, though I still never gave up hope.

In the meantime, as well as the coal shed, I'd now found a second safe place to hide in the garden, in the shade of a tree down the side of the house. Whenever I could, I would sit and play with my only doll in one of these spots, and if Ronald came looking for me, I would duck down, holding my breath so as not to make a sound, even though he could not have heard me. It delighted me to think he could not see me because of his failing eyesight, and although I would pay dearly for those moments when I later went back into the house, somehow it always seemed worth it.

SIX

Running Scared

The excitement amongst pupils and staff alike was almost palpable as the school's brand-new swimming pool neared completion. It had been the sole topic of conversation for weeks, as everyone wanted to play a part in the display that was to mark the grand opening. I'd learnt to swim at a very young age during trips to the local lido with my mum, dad and brother, and although I had not been back since being snatched away by Ronald, my swimming skills were still advanced for someone my age, so there was every possibility I would be chosen to play a prominent part – and so it proved.

Those of us who were selected were taken around the new building in the days leading up to the occasion, but on entering the changing-rooms, I was gripped by terror when I realised that I would have to undress in front of everyone else. All sorts of images involving Ronald flooded my mind, and the mere notion of my classmates seeing my naked body made me feel physically sick. It was already quite clear they regarded me as different from them, as shown in the way the 'pack' had instinctively ostracised me, but surely if they caught a glimpse of me naked they would spot some sign of my secret shame? The teachers didn't question my reason for suddenly wanting to be excused from taking part in the display, and from that day on I regularly forged letters to get myself out of swimming and games, just to avoid the horror that was the communal changing-rooms. The adults in my life didn't seem to notice – certainly Ronald and Emily never came to any parent–teacher evenings, read letters about forthcoming events or even questioned why I never brought home a school report – but my schoolmates were far more perceptive. They soon twigged I was skiving all forms of PE, and it became just another excuse for them to bully the 'Dummies' Kid'.

The trips into town to go shopping with my birth-parents became increasingly embarrassing for me as I became ever more aware of passers-by staring at us in the street, but the most lasting humiliation was caused by the items we bought, which only provided more fuel for the school bullies. My clothes had already made me a target, as I so rarely wore new ones, but on those occasions when Ronald deemed it necessary for me to have new items, he would always insist they be large enough to last whilst I grew into them. This is quite a common practice for frugal parents, but my new clothes were always several sizes too large and would literally hang in folds from my body, much to the delight of my classroom tormentors. Perhaps I should have taken some comfort in the fact that he had not singled me out for this peculiar punishment, as he enforced the same rules on Emily, and she was long past the age where she might grow into new clothes. I remember one bright-pink coat he bought her that might well have looked nice on a woman twice her size, but it was going cheap in a sale and that was all that mattered. Needless to say, Ronald's appearance was always immaculate: he took great care to dress smartly whenever he went out and would always be dressed in the smartest shirt, tie and jacket, with perfectly ironed trousers and highly polished shoes.

As the daily misery of life continued, and I faced regular night-time terrors at the hands of my birth-father, the only place I was able to hide was inside my head, where my tormentors couldn't reach me. There, I still dreamed of my lost family, and as the desperation to see Mum, whom I had not heard from since the day they all waved goodbye to me from the car, grew ever stronger, I decided to take matters into my own hands and write to her. My chance came when I spotted both Ronald and Emily out in the garden one afternoon. My heart was racing as I rummaged through Ronald's writing desk to find his personal address book and hurriedly scribbled down the address and phone number on a scrap of paper I'd torn from my school exercise book. Heaven knows what punishment I would have received if I'd been caught but, emboldened by the fact that I could still see them in the garden, I continued to look through this private drawer to see what I could find. Hidden at the back of the desk, I discovered the red container in which they collected their loose change. It was subdivided into different-sized sections to hold half-crowns, shillings and sixpences through to pennies and halfpennies and, without thinking of the consequences, I snatched a handful so I could buy a stamp and envelope.

The days turned into weeks as I waited for the sound of the postman each morning, desperately hoping that I'd spot an envelope with my mum's handwriting on it. In the letter, I had begged her to come and get me, saying I would never stop crying until she did, but with each batch of post I reached before Ronald had the chance to sift through it my heart sank that little bit lower, as I never heard back. Perhaps Ronald had managed to intercept it, but to me it felt as though I had been forgotten and abandoned by my family. To compensate, I began making return trips to the writing desk, and it seemed so easy to pilfer small amounts each time that I thought neither Ronald nor Emily would ever discover my little thefts. I would buy pencils, colouring books and other small items, explaining to my birth-parents that friends at school had given them to me, which served not only to cover up my crime but also to make me feel special and wanted in some way, even if my generous friends were imaginary.

I didn't see or hear Emily approach me from behind the day she caught me red-handed, but I heard her scurry off to the garden to get Ronald, and my heart pounded in my chest as I waited for the inevitable. As he stormed into the room, I knew I'd be shown no mercy, and soon his bony fingers were digging into my arms as he shook me with such force I thought my eyes would pop out of my skull. All the while he was bellowing how wicked and evil I was and that God would punish me, although with everything that had happened to me I thought He already was.

I was ordered to sit on the floor as Ronald left the room and then returned with every item of clothing I had and the sewing kit. He then told me I had to sew up all the pockets with thick white cotton, using large stitches so they were easily visible, to ensure that I could not put anything in them again. The following day, he dragged me into school and there before the class made me translate as he told the teacher and pupils what I'd done. I don't remember what the teacher said, but I remember the faces of the other children looking up at me, some sniggering and whispering to one another, while others just stared at my grunting birth-father, who swayed unsteadily as he gesticulated.

This was a cruel and humiliating punishment, and removed any ounce of pleasure I still got from going to school, but it did nothing to deter me from stealing from the drawer. Instead, it only taught me to be more careful.

For it was then that I first began to run away, and I needed their loose change to fund my little excursions. It didn't matter where I went as long as I was out of that house, although I always made sure I got back at the right time so that my absence wouldn't be noticed. I also used to pretend that I was still going to church on Sundays, but instead I'd use the collection money I'd been given, and any other coins I'd managed to accumulate, to buy sweets and fizzy drinks before setting off for the recreation ground. I loved it at the rec, and for those few hours I enjoyed a taste of freedom that was far sweeter than the confectionery I chewed on. I would go higher and higher on the swings, twisting the chains around and around before letting them go and spinning in a jerky circle with my eyes shut, shedding all thoughts of that house and him. Occasionally, I would meet children there from the other side of the village. They knew nothing about me or my parents, and we would hang out together, playing in the small coppice at the back of the rec. During the warm summer months, I would sit contentedly watching people playing tennis in the courts up by the big posh houses, wondering what it must be like to live their seemingly carefree lives. I promised myself that one day I would live in a grand house, too.

As I became a bit bolder, my escapes became progressively more adventurous, and on several occasions I ran a few miles away to my mum's eldest sister, Aunt Lily. The first time was during the summer holidays, and when I refused to go back, social services actually intervened and allowed me to stay for a couple of weeks as a sort of holiday and to give my birth-parents a break. For me, it was like a dream come true, as not only did I enjoy the kindness of my aunt and uncle but my older cousin Alison, who was married now with three children of her own, only lived a few doors away, and for the first time in so long I felt as if I were truly a part of a family again.

I also learnt more valuable life lessons in those few weeks than I did in all the time I would spend with my birth-parents. Aunt Lily had a lodger staying with her who was the first black person I'd ever met. He was very kind to me, and I would sit in attentive silence as he spoke to me for hours about his home in Trinidad, painting wonderfully vivid pictures of a distant and exotic land. One day he came home from work with his hand dripping blood, and I could not stop staring at the deep cut as Aunt Lily cleaned it and bound it up, for underneath his black skin the flesh was pink, just like mine. Aunt Lily spotted me staring and gave me a stern look before telling me to go out into the garden and play. Later, she sat me down and explained that everyone was the same under their skin, no one was better or worse, just different on the outside. I have never forgotten that talk with her, and it made an impression that has lasted with me to this day.

During that first trip, I made friends with some local children, who, like those at the rec, didn't know my family history. I was in my element climbing the trees with them and ignored the warnings of my aunt, who was worried I would fall and hurt myself. I was too busy enjoying myself to listen and, in an attempt to impress my new-found friends, I decided to try climbing the tallest tree of all. At a point part of the way up, a soft rotten bough collapsed beneath me and I lost my footing, but instead of falling straight to the ground, I seemed to slide down the tree's gnarled trunk, unaware at first that part of the broken bough had cut into my arm. On hitting the ground, I became aware of a searing pain scorching the underside of my arm, and the blood seeping from the wound was already threatening to stain my summer frock. It wasn't the pain or the shock at seeing the blood that brought uncontrollable tears to my eyes, however, it was the prospect of telling Auntie Lily, who would surely be so angry she'd send me back to Ronald and Emily straight away. This fear stung me into action, and I composed myself sufficiently on the way back to take my socks off and wrap them tightly around my bleeding arm.

Auntie Lily was in the front room watching television when I got back, so I slipped past unnoticed and went straight to bed. When she came upstairs to check on me, I pretended I'd already fallen asleep, but as soon as I heard my aunt and uncle go to bed, I crept out silently from my own and tiptoed to the bathroom to check on the damage in the mirror. I was horrified to see the large cut under my arm and the bruised and grazed skin all red and blue, but at least it was no longer bleeding so profusely. I tried, unsuccessfully, to scrub the blood out of my socks in the sink, and my heart sank as I realised I'd have to tell my aunt in the morning what I'd done. As I wrapped the socks back around my arm and returned to bed for a restless night, I feared the worst.

Aunt Lily eyed me suspiciously when I came down to breakfast and asked me why I'd gone straight to bed without any supper the night before. I burst into tears as I showed her my arm, begging her not to send me home and promising not to disobey her again. She did tell me off as I deserved but also put a soothing arm around me as she promised she wouldn't send me home early then dressed my arm and put my socks in to soak.

Aunt Lily's kindness was, however, merely a reprieve, as the holiday came to an end all too soon for my liking and I returned to my birth-parents' home. I was back in the world of endless chores and knocking on doors to get orders for Ronald's baskets. I'd also returned to the regular beatings and nightly visits.

I thought of my happy days with Aunt Lily and her family all the time, and I continued to run away at every opportunity, but Ronald's patience was wearing thin. On one occasion after I fled to my aunt's, Emily and Ronald were at the door within a matter of hours, as they knew they'd find me there. They were both absolutely livid and seemed to relish telling Aunt Lily what a dreadful problem I was and what a truly wicked girl I was growing up to be. The twisted snarl on Ronald's lips told me all I needed to know about what lay in store for me, and this time he couldn't even wait until we were all safely behind closed doors. This was most unusual for him, as, being the clever, sly, manipulative man he was, he was always careful to show his 'holier than thou' or 'pity poor me' face in public, but a neighbour later told my aunt that as soon as my birth-parents had walked me to the end of the road and entered the little alleyway that divided the houses, he turned on me. The neighbour couldn't decipher his guttural threats, but she witnessed him shouting, pushing and slapping me as he dragged me down the alleyway. This was nothing, though, compared to the prolonged beating I received back at the house or the night-time assault that followed, when he hurt me in ways no normal adult could imagine.

It was during this period that I first found methods other than drifting off into my daydreams to alleviate my anguish. Locked in the bathroom, I would reach for Ronald's razor and drag its sharp edge across my arms, or, hidden in my bedroom, I would carve deep marks on my wrists with the point of a safety pin. For some reason, these episodes of self-harm made me feel somehow more alive. Initially, I was careful not to draw too much blood, and even in the warmest of weather I always wore long sleeves to hide my scars. Soon I became addicted to the strange relief these self-inflicted wounds offered me, and there were many times I needed a bandage to cover up my handiwork. I would claim I'd simply fallen over and hurt my wrist, and no one, least of all Ronald and Emily, ever questioned this.

A vague notion began forming in my mind, one I became increasingly unable to ignore. What if I cut my wrists deeply enough and let all the hurt flow out of me along with the blood in my veins? My death would release not only Ronald and Emily from the burden of bringing up such an evil daughter but also free me from the hollow emptiness of my life. It seemed like such a simple solution. I slipped into the bathroom and didn't hesitate as I reached for Ronald's razor, calmly removing the blade with ease. At the first cut to my wrist, I marvelled at the bubbles of blood created on my skin but, try as I might, I just couldn't slice deeply enough through to the main vein as I was overcome with pain. I washed my wrist under the cold tap until the water turned from scarlet to a faded pink, then dried and bandaged my arm before cleaning and replacing Ronald's blade. Looking back, this was my first suicide attempt, and I wasn't even in my teens. It certainly wouldn't be my last.

SEVEN

From Pillar to Post

The butterflies in my stomach were for once not all that unpleasant. I wasn't too sure what my new home would be like, but I packed my belongings into a battered old suitcase with a certain sense of anticipation rather than apprehension. Just weeks after my 12th birthday, a decision had been made that my birth-parents could supposedly no longer cope with my wayward behaviour, and I was to be taken into care. With hindsight, it seems very odd that Ronald would be prepared to relinquish the power he'd obviously enjoyed over me within his home, but I will never know for certain whether my birth-mother played some part in this move, which she perhaps hoped would be for my own good. Whoever made the decision to inform the social services about my situation soon became irrelevant, as all I knew in my heart was that this might just yet prove to be a happier time for me.

On my first day, the house mother gave me a guided tour of my new surroundings, and I instantly liked what I saw. At the front of the building was a large room where the children could entertain visitors, and nearby were the dining room and kitchen, from where homely cooking smells would waft throughout the building. At the back were the schoolrooms, which seemed less imposing than at my old school, and a further room that acted as the children's common room. We were encouraged to decorate this room the way we wished, and I soon started to enjoy joining in with the others to paint the walls in bright colours and create vivid murals with wild psychedelic patterns on them resembling Pink Floyd album covers, although to my knowledge none of us were on drugs! There was a television and a record player for our entertainment and lots of big soft scatter cushions on the floor as well as large comfortable sofas and tables and chairs. It was all far more inviting than my birth-parents' home, and we children loved and cared for our own room with a real sense of pride.

On arrival, my suitcase didn't contain many clothes, as Ronald's rigid budgeting had never allowed for the luxury of a fashionable wardrobe for his daughter. I could therefore hardly contain my surprise and delight when I was shown to a cupboard full of second-hand but good-quality clothes and told to take my pick. It was as if all my Christmases had come at once as I chose a short grey miniskirt, the first I'd ever owned, and a multicoloured top with long trumpet-shaped sleeves. I was extremely proud of my new clothes, and they made me feel very grown up,

Away from my birth-parents, and especially Ronald, I no longer had to endure the regular night-time abuse, and the weight this lifted from my young shoulders was immeasurable. Neither of them even came to visit me, so I felt completely free to be myself. The other children at the home all had problems of their own, but we never discussed the reasons we were there, and they seemed to accept me. I made a lot of friends for the first time, and it was during my stay there that I enjoyed an innocent introduction to make-up, new hairstyles and boys. Despite all I had experienced at the hands of my birth-father, I was in fact very naive when it came to boys my own age. I had no idea about the facts of life, and when I heard the older girls talking about things they did with their boyfriends, I would try to eavesdrop. I never told anyone about what Ronald had done to me, and still didn't really understand it. It felt wrong, but I didn't know why. I had no idea whether the same thing happened to other people and this was just something that some men did to you.

But while I may have been growing up, my time in the home was also an opportunity to enjoy some carefree childhood experiences, something that had been denied me for the past five years. Unlike some of my new friends, I even enjoyed the household chores, at which we all took turns, such as laying and clearing the dinner tables and tidying the rooms. Without exception, everyone enjoyed the occasional day trips to the seaside or to museums, and the coach journeys were filled with children's riotous laughter both to and from our destinations. I particularly loved the long summer evenings when we played rounders after school in the big field at the back of the home.

However, whilst my memories of the home were all good, others were not so lucky. The staff bedroom was at the end of the corridor on the level we all slept on, and whoever was house mother or father at any given time would sleep there. Almost all of our guardians were wonderful and kind, but there was one house father all the boys were frightened of. He would call boys individually to his room at night after all the lights had been switched off and, while none of the children ever spoke about it – young victims have a habit of keeping these secrets to themselves – we all somehow understood what was going on.

Despite my safer and happier surroundings, I still yearned to be back with my mum, dad and brother, and in my quiet moments my mind would still wander wistfully off to our happy times together, such as the days out we had in Dad's old car. Mum would invariably pack a wonderful picnic for us all to enjoy when we reached our destination, and my cousins and I would tuck into it gratefully after hours of playing together. On one occasion, we found a particularly lovely spot with a big expanse of grass and several large oak trees to shelter us from the hot summer sun. Mum laid out the rug and set about preparing our meal, boiling water on a little stove and buttering the thick slices of bread we all loved, while the rest of us played cricket. It was a blisteringly hot day, and Mum soon called us all to eat, but as we lay on the rug, two men approached us and Dad went over to meet them. We couldn't hear the conversation, but when Dad came back he seemed a little flustered and, despite our protests, said we had to leave immediately. As we were all bundled very quickly into the car, Dad explained the need for a hasty getaway. It seemed the two men had been watching us for some time, as it turned out we had accidentally been trespassing. Not only that, the scenic spot we'd chosen for our picnic just happened to be part of the garden belonging to the Prime Minister — we'd been playing cricket on the grounds of Chequers! As we set off, Mum and Dad began laughing loudly in the front of the car, and whilst we children didn't fully understand what had gone on, their laughter was infectious and we joined in from the back seats, giggling all the way home.

Having become so settled at the children's home, I'd begun to regard my stay there as permanent, but towards the end of the summer it was decided I would go into foster care with a family a few miles away. This certainly wasn't my choice, and as the day for me to leave loomed ever closer, I became increasingly sad and frightened about what lay in store. Just the thought of the upheaval of leaving the children's home was worrying enough, but what if my new foster parents didn't like me? What if my foster father was like Ronald and would creep into my bed each night?

With a very heavy heart, I was escorted by a social worker to my new home, my legs becoming lead weights as I walked towards it. As we stood at the bottom of the steep drive, I looked up at the black-and-white-fronted house up on the hill, with its dark windows and criss-crossed diamond leadwork. When we reached the big black door, with its sombre black knocker, my legs turned to jelly and my tongue felt thick and furry in my dry mouth, but I forced back the tears welling up in my eyes, as I was determined not to let anyone see me cry.

After a few moments, the heavy front door creaked open and there stood a tall thin woman with long dark hair. She glanced at me and smiled but did not say a word, speaking instead only to the social worker before I was ushered into what I later discovered was the library. There, sitting by the fire, was my foster father, similarly tall and dark-haired, and he briefly flicked his eyes over me as he spoke with the social worker whilst I stood silently by, not listening to the drone of the adults' conversation, just waiting patiently to be told what to do next. As the social worker made to leave, my foster mother took me by the hand and led me upstairs to see my new room and unpack my belongings. She said she would ring a bell when dinner was ready, and I should then come down and meet the family. With that, I was left alone.

I surveyed my new surroundings, taking in the dark beams overhead and the small windows that made the room seem very dark and cold. An eerie silence hung all around as I unpacked my few belongings. Peering through the window into the garden, I spotted two small children playing. I watched them for a while before sitting silently on my bed and waiting for the dinner bell to ring. I kicked my heels as the minutes dragged, and then suddenly the bell rang out through the silence. My heart was in my mouth again as I descended the stairs to find them all sitting at the dining-room table. After introducing me to the children, my foster parents indicated my seat with a nod of their heads, and throughout the course of the meal not another word was said to me by anyone at the table. I felt very much the invisible outsider who quite clearly did not belong at this family gathering, and it was a feeling that grew with each passing day. My foster family were in no way cruel to me, there were no beatings or night-time visits. I simply lived in their home, but I was not a member of their family, and I yearned to be away from this perpetual gloom and back at the children's home with my friends.

It was still the summer holidays, and as I only had a few household chores to do, I spent much of my time alone reading in the corner of my room. Other hours were frittered away standing at the front gate watching the world go by on the busy road outside. It was during this time that I first noticed the man who often drove past in his truck. He had gingery fair hair and a huge smile, and I was thrilled when he started waving to me. I started to look forward to him driving by each day, as it made me feel special – it felt as if he was looking out for me as much as I was for him.

But even with this distraction I couldn't hide from the fact that I was soon due to start a new school. I was terrified as a result of my past experiences, and my fears proved well founded. As I was so far behind in my studies, it wasn't long before I was frequently being hauled up in front of the class to write out my mistakes on the blackboard. Once again, this, and the fact that I was a foster child, gave my more vicious classmates ample ammunition with which to bully me, and I soon dreaded school as much as I had previously done. I tried my old trick of forging letters to get me out of PE, but this time the teachers refused to accept them and would check up on me. The only way I could avoid the communal showers therefore seemed to be to bunk off as often as I could. It wasn't long before my foster parents discovered this, but while they were absolutely furious with me, still they never struck me. Sometimes I wish they had beaten me, as at least it would have meant there was some physical contact between us, and I began to feel increasingly neglected as I watched them cuddle and play with their own children.

On the morning I was next due to have PE, I stood in the bathroom before leaving the house, desperately trying to think of a way out. Then, as I put the toothpaste back in the cupboard, I spotted a dark brown bottle hidden on the top shelf at the back, so I climbed up and took it down. The oval-shaped bottle was ridged on one side, and I was fascinated by the skull-and-crossbones symbol on its label. I unscrewed the lid and took a sniff, the noxious odour making my eyes water. This convinced me I'd found something poisonous, so I slipped it into my coat pocket and left for school as usual. I ambled down the road away from the house, but when I came to the T-junction, I took the opposite turning from the one that led to school and headed off through a wooded area. I walked and walked that damp autumnal day, fingering the cool glass of the bottle in my pocket as I went, and my mind raced over the consequences if I were to drink its contents. As darkness started to fall, I looked through the windows of the houses I passed and spotted televisions flickering or families sitting down to eat their evening meal. This only served to make me feel utterly alone and helpless, as I had no such home to go to where I would be warmly welcomed. I felt neither tired nor hungry as I trudged the streets, my mind now focused only on drinking the poison and ending my misery. My thoughts were interrupted, however, when a police car pulled up alongside me. Back at the station, the bottle was taken from me, but I never revealed why I had been carrying it. I had already learnt to say and do what I believed people wanted me to. After I had spent some time in a cell, my foster parents arrived to collect me. Nothing was said, no questions were asked, and we simply drove home in silence.

Soon after this, however, and much to my delight I began bumping into my truck-driver friend on my walks to school. At first, he just waved and smiled his big friendly smile, but then he began stopping to talk to me. Often he would pull up, push open his cab door and ask how I was this fine morning or tell me how pretty I looked today. It made me feel so special, loved even, so when one day he asked me if I'd like to go for a ride, I didn't hesitate, and in an instant I'd climbed up into the cab next to him. Off we went down the country lanes, and I felt so grown up viewing the world from the high vantage point of the cab while my new friend asked me questions about myself and paid me the sweetest compliments. I told him I lived with foster parents but that I didn't like it there as they were so unfriendly, so when he parked in a lay-by and told me to sit closer to him so he could give me a cuddle, I complied without question. It felt so good to have someone hug me, and I felt safe in his big strong arms.

We met again a few days later and off we went down the same secluded country lanes before pulling up in the lay-by. I felt so warm and happy inside as he put his arms around me for another hug, so much so I didn't even flinch when he guided my hand onto his crotch or when he undid his zip and took his penis out. He seemed to love and care for me, and I craved that so badly I would have done anything he said. I had no idea that I had the right to say no, and again I just thought that this was something that men did.

Our meetings continued, and each time he wanted to do more, telling me it was because I was such a wonderful girl and so special to him. It didn't hurt even when I allowed him to penetrate me. It was so different from when Ronald had forced himself upon me from behind, as this man was so gentle and kind. I had no notion that he was abusing me, as I felt truly loved.

'Izzy! Izzy, get down from there at once!' My foster father's shouts cut through the chilly morning air just as I was about to climb into the cab, having met my truck-driver friend again as arranged. I dutifully stepped down onto the pavement and heard the cab door slam behind me before the lorry drove off at speed. I never saw the driver again. I soon learnt that my foster father had spotted me getting out of the truck on the previous occasion, and when I left the house that morning, he'd decided to follow me so as to catch me at it.

My social worker was called, my bags were packed and by teatime I was back in the children's home. I must have told someone what we had done in the lorry as I was told that this kind of behaviour was unacceptable – yet as an adult I can now only question why no alarm bells rang and why no one thought it strange I was sexually active at the age of 12.

I remained at the home for the next few weeks, happy to be reunited with my friends there and away from my cold and unloving foster parents. But this happiness wouldn't last, as another foster home was found for me on the far side of Luton, well away from my first foster parents. Once again my bags were packed and off I went. The family were very nice and they had a three-year-old daughter who had the most beautiful white-blonde hair. She liked me playing with her and her toys, and I was only too happy to join in, for I was still a child myself. Having been the youngest among my cousins, I had never had a younger sibling to play with, and I found that I really enjoyed it.

However, no matter how friendly and loving my second foster parents were to me, I was increasingly desperate to be reunited with my mum. On one occasion, she was asked to come to a meeting that social services called to discuss my future. I remember that she brought me some new shoes and I begged her to speak to the social worker and make them let me come home with her. But her request to have me live with her was refused and, in frustration, my behaviour started to spiral further out of control.

At the back of the house where my foster parents lived, there was a large park that was used when travelling fairgrounds came to town. I remember being fascinated by the lights and music and the squeals of half-fear, half-delight coming from the people on the rides. I would hang around there a lot on my own, and one day I met a group of four or five young men. They were hanging around the rides, and I was aware of them watching me. As I moved to watch the next ride, they followed, and eventually one of them came over and spoke, while the others hung back a little.

We chatted away about the fair, and he told me he worked in a restaurant in the town. He was dressed in a white shirt and tight white jeans with shiny patent shoes. I thought he was very good looking with his shoulder-length dark hair, and I was thrilled when he took me on some of the rides and brought me candyfloss, which I had never had before.

The others eventually drifted away, saying something to him that I didn't understand; but I wasn't worried, I was just enjoying myself and felt very grown up in the man's company. I should think he was in his early to mid-twenties, and I didn't tell him my real age.

We started to walk along with his arm around my shoulder, and then at some point he kissed me. I didn't like it or dislike it; it was just what happened when you were with a man, that's what they wanted to do. I didn't know I had a choice; I just did what he seemed to want me to do.

We went over to some bushes, out of sight of the fair, and he pulled me down onto the ground. I let him undo my clothes and made no move to stop him. I remember him talking, but I didn't understand what he was saying, and then he was on top of me and inside me. After it was over, he quickly stood up and straightened his clothes while I fumbled around with mine. Before this happened, he had said he was going to take me on the big wheel, but now he said he had to go back to work. He turned and pushed his way out of the bushes and was gone, leaving me still sitting on the ground alone and confused.

I went home as if nothing had happened, and the following day I went back to the park looking for him but couldn't find him. I remember crying, not because I felt used, as I didn't understand that was what had happened. I just thought I had done something wrong and he didn't like me any more. Now I understand that as a child I was craving human contact, which I confused with love.

I also started to run away again, not for just a day like before but for two or three days at a time. I was still in touch with a girl I'd met at the children's home and, as I no longer cared what was going to happen to me, the pair of us would hitch lifts in lorries all over the country, getting ourselves into dangerous situations with lorry drivers until inevitably we were picked up by the police. My second set of foster parents finally conceded they couldn't cope with me, and once more I was sent back to the children's home.

It was during this third spell at the home that Emily and Ronald started to visit me for the first time since they'd handed me over. At first, the meetings in the room reserved for guests were particularly awkward, but in time we all relaxed, and in some strange way I felt happy to see them, as they were both being so nice to me. Their visits became more and more frequent until eventually my social worker decided I should go back to live with them on a trial basis. I didn't object, and as they had moved to a different house on the northern outskirts of Luton, I was quite looking forward to seeing their new home. Without the memories of the last house hanging over me, it seemed like a fresh start for us all.

This move, however, also entailed me starting yet another new school and, as ever, it was a nightmare. I was always the new girl, always different from the rest, and I never felt as if I fitted in. My work was by now so far behind that I started to resort to all sorts of ruses in order to avoid being unmasked as the class dunce. I would lose books, forget to hand in homework or try to copy work over a classmate's shoulder, all of which made me even more unpopular. I started to forge letters again, whether they were for getting out of games lessons, explaining away non-existent doctor's and dentist's appointments or for days when I was supposedly ill at home. Fortunately for me, no one in authority seemed too inclined to check up on me this time.

Life at my birth-parents' new home was quite bearable at first: neither of them beat me as they had before and nor was I subjected to Ronald's night-time visits. There were no signs of affection but no aggression either, and while I resumed my chores, such as sorting out his canes and getting orders for him, Ronald would make what for him was cordial conversation, such as suggesting he would buy me a car when I grew up so I could drive him around and look after him. However, it was not to last and, having learnt at the children's home to sleep soundly in my bed free from fear, I was woken with a start when he did finally climb back into my bed. As his rough hands grabbed for me and I smelt his rancid breath, all the old fears came rushing to the surface and in a moment of panic I said I would tell Emily if he did not leave me alone. It was my first show of defiance towards him, and I felt a fleeting sense of satisfaction as he backed away. But even as he closed the bedroom door behind him, I knew I had no choice but to run away again.

EIGHT

Homeward Bound

The rain had been pouring incessantly for days, but I couldn't let this deter me; my mind was set and tonight was the night. I lay under the covers until I heard Emily and Ronald retire for the night before tiptoeing across the bedroom floor and easing the window open, careful not to make a sound, as they were very sensitive to vibrational noise. I felt the rainwater soak through my clothes as I perched on the sodden windowsill before closing my eyes, holding my breath and leaping for freedom. The glare of the streetlights lit up the puddles all around but, pulling my sodden coat ever tighter around me in a vain attempt to shield myself from the rain, I was careful to stay in the shadows for fear of a passing police car spotting me. Thirty minutes later, I'd paid for my ticket at the train station with the handful of coins I'd dug from the deep corners of my coat pockets and boarded the train to Cambridge. I sat in the corner of the carriage and tried not to look too conspicuous to my fellow passengers. I was a 12-year-old girl travelling alone at night, and my heart beat so hard as I stared out of the window into the darkness that I was sure everyone else could hear it.

The relentless rain followed me all the way to Cambridge and it fell in sheets from the station roof as I climbed down onto the platform and made my way to the exit. There, people stood huddled under umbrellas as they waited in line for a taxi, and one couple asked me where I was headed. I told them the name of the village where my mum and dad lived, and they kindly offered to take me in their cab, as they were headed for the next village on from where my mum and dad ran their shop. After setting off, however, we found out that all roads leading into the village were flooded, as the deluge had caused the river to burst its banks. I was so near yet so far. The taxi driver and the other passengers discussed the problem amongst themselves, and after a hasty call to my mum and dad from a phone box, it seemed the driver had found the solution. We walked across several fields and a swollen stream before we eventually found ourselves at the bottom of my parents' garden, and there stood my dad, reaching out for my hand. There too was my mum; she hugged me long and hard then shook me with a frown on her face before hugging me all over again. I was a sorry sight, drenched through to the skin with my bare legs cut by brambles and covered in a stinging nettle rash, but I was home at last and nothing else mattered.

There wasn't a lot of living space above the shop, as my parents and brother Robert, who was by now a teenager and very grown up, shared it with Mum's brother Harry, his wife Ann and her daughter Susan.

My uncle made it quite clear from the start he wasn't happy with me being there, but he agreed to let me stay, and somehow, I'm not sure quite how, Mum also persuaded the authorities to allow me to stay. I slept on a put-you-up in their room, and I couldn't have been happier.

The days after the flood were rather disorientating as I tried to get used to my new surroundings whilst also doing my bit to help clear up after the damage the floodwaters had caused. The day after my arrival, I took a peek at the cellar, as I'd been told that the butter, fats, bottles of pop, vegetables and bundling sticks were stored down there because it was so cold. It was also where Dad would hang the bacon in a special cage before jointing it on a table ready for boiling. It sounded like an Aladdin's Cave of goodies, but on my first view it was more like a giant stew, with all sorts of goods bobbing around in the water.

The damage from the flood was not only physical but also financial for my parents and their business partners, as everything except the kindling wood had to be thrown away. Once the cellar had been pumped out, it became my responsibility to take the wood out into the yard and keep turning each piece over in the sunshine in the hope it would dry the sticks out sufficiently. It seemed to take forever to count and tie the successfully dried sticks into bundles, but I did it willingly, as not only did it make me feel I had played my part in the clean-up process but I also hoped it would please my Uncle Harry, who on top of the flood damage could barely tolerate me being there.

I did everything and anything around the shop and

house to show myself willing, including getting all the boxed orders together before going out with Dad on his deliveries. These were particularly fun times and especially so in the spring of the following year, when Dad would let me sit beside him with the van's sliding door wide open so I could watch the passing countryside as we drove along, the fields full of the new season's lambs and cavorting calves. I also loved helping out in the shop, whether I was decorating the windows or changing the stock under Mum's guidance, but I made a point of keeping away from my uncle at all times, as to him I quite clearly remained the cuckoo in the nest.

To complicate matters further, a nagging resentment lurked beneath the surface of my apparent happiness. I was totally unaware that Dad was ill, and had been for some time, with severe back pains that the doctors had warned would most likely leave him confined to a wheelchair. This was the reason that he and the family had moved away to go into business with my uncle in the first place, as my parents saw it as the only way they would both be able to work and keep a roof over their heads. I was also unaware of the efforts my mum had made to take me with them, only to be rebuffed by the authorities, who believed that my place was with Ronald and Emily. Mum had had no other option but to make the choices she did, but it seemed to me that I had simply been discarded, and I had felt for so long that I was unloved and worthless.

I couldn't tell my parents about what Ronald and the others had done to me; these were my wicked secrets, and I believed that I deserved what had happened because Ronald had drummed it into me that I was evil and that bad things only happened to you if you were wicked. Whether I liked it or not, I felt that everything had irrevocably changed since we were last all together. I was no longer a naive seven year old; I was now thirteen and far from innocent any more. I never would have wanted to deliberately hurt the parents I loved so dearly, but my confused state of mind began manifesting itself in some unacceptable behaviour. Whether it was to punish my parents for leaving me or to punish myself I will never know, but I remember that on more than one occasion I wrapped up my own faeces in toilet paper and hid it in the vast bottom drawer of the large wardrobe in my parents' bedroom. Although the drawer was not often used, Mum must surely have found these deposits, though she never mentioned it to me.

It was during this time at that shop that I started having my periods. I had no idea what was happening to me the first time I saw the blood on my knickers and thought I must be dying because of the pain in my stomach. After it continued for a couple of days, I eventually told my mum what had happened and, while seeming slightly embarrassed, she got me some sanitary towels from one of the top shelves in the shop and told me it was nothing to worry about; it was just something that happened to all women when you grew up. Later that night, she sat me down and tried to explain to me about the facts of life, but I was mortified and told her that I already knew about all that. Unfortunately, I was lying, and all I knew was the overheard gossip I'd picked up at the children's home.

Another new school presented the same old problems

of showering and changing with everyone else during games lessons, and on the whole I still found making friends very difficult. But to some of the kids I did have an appeal, purely because I lived above a shop. They urged me to get them free pop, sweets and cigarettes, which I did willingly, stealing from my own family in order to be accepted and liked by my peers. My coat had rather wide pockets on each side and, having pulled the inside stitches apart, I would regularly fill up the lining with stolen goods for my new friends. Ironically, there was also a feel-good factor to some of my thefts, as I had befriended a girl at school who lived with her poor grandmother in a filthy little house in the town centre. I went there one lunchtime and, after witnessing such poverty first-hand, it struck me as totally unfair that they should have so little when we had so much back at the shop. I began stealing tins of soup and other items which I would take to the grandmother in my lunch breaks, and it made me feel happy to see her so grateful.

Meanwhile, during the school day I had discovered that the best way to get out of doing things I didn't like was to be a bit of a clown. This also helped increase my standing amongst some of the pupils, as everyone – except the teacher – seemed to enjoy the way I could disrupt the class by making them laugh. The downside was that I either spent a lot of time sitting outside the classroom as yet another exasperated teacher sent me from their lesson, or I was sent to the headmaster to have my open palms slapped with his ruler. These slaps may have grazed the surface, but they couldn't even touch the pain I felt inside, so it was all too easy to block out the punishments and continue with my clowning around as before.

This devil-may-care attitude earned me quite a reputation and, as my behaviour deteriorated, I was soon welcomed into the older set of naughty children. I even started dating a boy old enough to be leaving school soon, although my mum remained blissfully unaware. I left each morning dressed as a typical schoolgirl, but on boarding the school bus and making my way to the back seat on the upper deck, I began the daily routine of rolling the top of my skirt over and over until it was as short as I dared before applying my make-up. Like so many other youngsters trying to act grown up, I also started smoking, and with cigarettes so readily available from the shop, I became even more popular within my circle of friends. However, it was while dressed in my amended school uniform and with a cigarette in my mouth that my uncle Harry caught me. He'd already had his suspicions over who was responsible for the missing stock in the shop and catching me smoking was the confirmation he needed. Much to my shame, he marched me back home, and I was sent upstairs whilst my future was decided.

A little while later, I was called back downstairs and, as the others sat in silence, Uncle Harry took the floor to tell me I was the black sheep of the family; he would not allow me to stay in the shop any longer, as he wanted nothing more to do with me; I must return to Ronald and Emily. Adopting the typical pose of a surly and angry adolescent, I pretended I didn't care and even said I actually wanted to go back to live with my birth-parents, but inside I was mortified. Why was I so bad all the time? It seemed that I'd become the very person that Ronald had always told me I was; he must have been right all along.

I returned in disgrace to my birth-parents with a particularly heavy heart, unsure what to expect, but little was said about my recent behaviour and life for the next few months was welcomingly uneventful. Ronald and Emily made few demands on me, and whatever spare time I had I spent with my old friends from the children's home.

During the Easter holidays, I met up with a few of my friends and we all decided we would have a party, which I perhaps somewhat foolishly suggested should be held at my birth-parents' house. To my surprise, Ronald and Emily agreed to my request, and on the evening of the party they retired to the room at the back of the house while I prepared some food and my friends began arriving with drinks. I warned my friends to keep things relatively quiet up until nine o'clock, as I knew that Ronald and Emily would go to bed then as they always did. True to form, Ronald popped his head around the door about nine and told me everyone was to be gone by ten o'clock. Not long after that, there was a knock at the front door and I let in Fred, the local skinhead and friend of one of my girlfriends. I was too busy enjoying myself to keep tabs on everyone, and I didn't spot Fred sneak into the back room, nor was I aware he'd stolen some money Ronald had left lying around in there. Ronald, however, must have sensed that something was not as he'd have wished, as he came charging down the stairs bellowing in his indecipherable manner. The sight of my birth-father wildly charging after Fred was enough to scare everyone else into fleeing the house and, despite the bravado I might have been displaying of late, I awaited Ronald's return with absolute dread.

The door slammed and his heavy footsteps made straight for the front room where I still sat. Without so much as a word, he grabbed a fistful of my hair and dragged me up the stairs. As he threw me onto my bed, I knew what was coming next. I struggled to free myself, but he began punching me repeatedly in the stomach until the wind was truly knocked out of me. I felt the room start spinning as I was on the verge of passing out. This time, as he forced himself inside me, I simply had no strength left to fight back.

The next day, I sat in silence as Ronald spoke with the social worker, who knew some sign language, in the front room, the scene of the previous evening's fun that now seemed so long ago. He told her I had stolen from him again, had organised a party in his house without permission and that I'd tried to hit him with an iron when he intervened, waving his arms all the while to illustrate his points. Once again, he trotted out his standard line about being a religious man from a long line of vicars who was at his wits' end having such an evil daughter. I saw nothing to be gained by defending myself, and perhaps I believed I deserved everything that happened to me, as after all I was indeed a thief and a liar. I let men touch me and I touched them; even my parents had finally washed their hands of me.

By lunchtime, I was back in the children's home, and I slipped straight back into my old routines. The cycle of lessons, chores and trips into town on a Saturday if I behaved suited me perfectly. One such Saturday, I went to the department store in town with one of my friends, and we amused ourselves by looking through all the make-up and earrings, holding them up to each other's ears to see what we looked like. The earrings were bright and dangly and just what we were looking for, but we had no intention of buying them, as we didn't have the money. I may have pilfered items from my parents' shop, but I'd never stolen from a big department store before. My friend had, though, and she explained what we had to do. But I was obviously not a fast learner, as we were both caught as we made to leave the shop and taken to the manager's office, where we hung our heads in shame as we waited for the police to arrive.

As the heavy cell door was locked behind me back at the station, I fought with all my might not to cry, but I couldn't stop shaking with fear, and the sobs soon followed. Quite a while later, I was told I had to make a statement, and as one male police officer asked me countless questions, his female colleague jotted down my answers. I was told to read the statement and sign my name at the bottom, but I was so frightened that I was unable to read any of the words. They all seemed to merge together on the page, so I merely pretended to read it and then signed it as I'd been told.

This was by no means to be the end of the matter, as I was sent to a remand centre whilst I awaited the date of my court appearance. The proceedings at the magistrates' court were little more than a blur, so many adults all discussing me at great length, and I didn't understand a word of it. Once it was over, my social worker explained that I'd been seen to be 'beyond the care and control of my parents' and found guilty as charged with aiding and abetting the other girl thief. I was to be sent away to an approved school.

NINE

The Prisoner

A cruel wind buffeted the car as we drove towards the imposing black wrought-iron gates, and I eyed the high brick wall that surrounded the school's perimeter with alarm. As the gates were opened and we drove through, I spotted a number of small houses along with a larger building that I presumed to be the school. I was escorted into one of the smaller buildings, where I was introduced to the matron and my new house mother, whose beady eyes fixed me with a piercing stare. My bag of possessions was then taken from me, and my house mother didn't utter a word as she escorted me to one of the smaller buildings. This was to be my new home, which I would share with seven other girls and this fearsome guardian by my side.

The house mother marched me through the building, which was deserted as my housemates were still in the school block, and on reaching the bathroom, I was ordered inside. I saw a number of toilet cubicles and sinks but only one bath with a wooden duckboard propped beside it. The bathroom was bitterly cold, and I shuddered when my house mother ordered me to strip and place my folded clothes on a chair that sat beside a cupboard in which towels were kept. She ignored me, however, turning instead to run the bath, so I fumbled nervously with my buttons as I began to remove the top half of my clothing, but I was still in my underwear when she next turned around.

'Have you got something to hide?' she barked at me. I mustered up the nerve to answer that I hadn't, but this didn't seem to placate her. 'I know you're trying to hide something, I can see it in your face,' she snarled as she ordered me to take off the rest of my clothes, all the while walking around me in a slow circle, looking me up and down and lifting my arms to check my armpits. 'Bend over and clasp your ankles,' she hollered, but I just couldn't bring myself to do it. Tears began burning the inside of my eyes, and every impulse in me ordered me to run. Then my house mother repeated her instruction, but this time in a low and menacing voice that frightened me so much I simply had to obey. Despite the shame I felt, I steadfastly refused to break down and cry in front of this woman. I was determined to do all I could not to show my fear of her.

I expected to feel her hands groping me at any moment, but it didn't happen; instead, she just looked at me silently as I maintained my humiliating position for what seemed an eternity. I felt she could see into the very core of me; she knew exactly what I was. Then she picked up my clothes and without adding so much as a drop more water to the lukewarm puddle that barely covered the bottom of the bath told me to get in and wash all over. I washed as quickly as I could, still shaking with fear and cold, and my house mother returned just as I was drying myself. On the chair she placed what was to be my uniform: a thin light-blue nylon overall with buttons down the front, a thin cardigan that would not keep me warm, long white socks and black slip-on plimsolls. Once I'd finished dressing, I followed her meekly as she took me on a tour of my new home, showing me the dormitory I was to sleep in and the rest of the upstairs, including her room, as well as the downstairs with its sitting room, dining room and kitchen areas.

Having been told the house rules, I was shown the rota board and was quite shocked to see my name was already on it; but just as she was explaining my duties, the outside door opened and in came the other seven girls with whom I would be sharing the house. The house mother called one of them forward, an older and bigger girl than me. I was informed that this was Tanya, the head girl, and I must do everything she told me. Tanya towered over me, her short dark hair bristling, and as I looked into her icy bright-blue eyes, I recognised the unmistakable hatred they contained. Just as experience had taught me to spot her potential for cruelty, she saw in me a victim, and I knew straightaway our paths would cross at some point.

The daily routine was as simple as it was repetitive: working in twos, we would take turns to lay and clear the breakfast tables in the mornings, having prepared the food itself, served the meal and poured the drinks. I was partnered with a girl called Mel and, as she was as unsure of her surroundings as I was, we hit it off instantly. Mel had only been sent to the approved school because she'd been caught continually bunking off school to get away from the bullies who tormented her there. It seemed to me like a case of out of the frying pan and into the fire. After breakfast, we were all escorted over to the school block, where we would remain for the rest of the day, having our main meal there, too. The schoolwork proved as problematic as ever, as I had missed so much of my studies over the years; but whilst I still felt stupid as I struggled with the most basic of tasks, I no longer cared if I succeeded or not. Just as the high walls of the school kept me imprisoned, I was building up a wall of my own between myself and everything that caused me pain.

At the end of each school day, our house mothers escorted us back to our individual houses, where we would be checked at the door to make sure we hadn't stolen anything from the school block. We then sat down to tea, which ran in the same manner as breakfast, with two girls laying the table and serving the rest. The girls' tables were over by the window opposite the kitchen door, and our house mother's table was in the corner at an angle, giving her the perfect vantage point from which to see everything that happened in the room.

The house mother missed nothing but nor did she intervene when the daily rounds of bullying took place. The worst perpetrators were Tanya and her hangers-on, and their acts of violence were often committed openly in front of the house mother. I learnt that Tanya had committed grievous bodily harm (amongst other crimes) and quickly realised that everyone lived in fear of her, perhaps even her hangers-on, scared that they too might become targets if they crossed her. It seemed to me that the house mother and the head girl were working in unison, both relishing the power they had over their charges, and neither of them missed a trick in exercising that control. The only difference I could see was that the house mother liked to bully the girls mentally whereas the head girl preferred physical bullying. For example, the house mother would not allow any form of privacy, and if you were having a bath or sitting on the toilet and she wanted to watch you wash or have a pee, then she would walk right in and stand there. The bathroom was also one of Tanya's favourite places to inflict torture, especially during the weekly bath nights, when we were also inspected for head and body lice. We would be ordered to bend over and clasp our ankles, as I had been on my first day, and if the head girl was present during the inspection, she would push her fingers into my anus and vagina, checking, she said, for anything I might be hiding there, as I was a thief. To my knowledge, this never happened to Mel – or at least she never confided in me that it had – but, whether I was being singled out or not, it served only to strip me of any last vestige of dignity. Just as at the hands of Ronald, I once more felt like a piece of meat. To me, the solution was simple: I might have nowhere to go, but I had at least to try to escape.

Adrenalin coursed through me as I lay in bed listening to the other girls' regular breathing, hoping they were by now fast enough asleep. As silently as I could, I then got up and tied my two bedsheets together. I then tied one end to the chest of drawers that sat next to the wall and threw the rest out of the window to the ground below. Our coats were kept downstairs, so all I had to keep me warm was my nightie, my nylon overall and my flimsy cardigan, and the night chill bit deeply as I climbed over the edge of the windowsill, holding firmly to the self-made rope I thought I'd be able to climb down. As I tried to descend, I lost my grip and fell straight down into the darkness, hitting the ground so hard in a crouching position that on impact the pain from my ankle ripped through me, causing me to fall sideways and bang my head. The pain was so intense that my entire body seemed almost to fizz, but through sheer force of will, I still managed to hobble to the wall and climb over before making my way down and across the road as quickly as I could. My brief moment of freedom was not to last, however, as I had not got very far before I was picked up by a police car. My heart sank as I saw its flashing blue light approaching, but I couldn't run from them as I could hardly walk. The officers informed me that the alarm had been raised almost immediately, so I never stood a chance.

I was driven straight back to the approved school, where both the matron and my house mother were waiting for me. The policemen told them they should probably get me to hospital to get my head and foot checked over and, before showing them out, the matron assured them I would be taken care of.

The matron didn't look at me when she came back in; instead, she repeated the order to my house mother to take care of me and went back to her bed. With the matron gone, my house mother strode towards me and kicked me straight on the ankle. The pain was like a shooting white light in front of my eyes, and I howled as I fell to the floor. 'We can take care of ourselves, can't we?' she hissed as she bent over me. 'You don't need to see a doctor, do you?' I did not dare argue with her, for I could not have coped if she'd kicked me again, so I hobbled to my feet and we made our way back to the house, where she followed me up the stairs and into the dormitory. I was not allowed so much as to sit down until I had untied the sheets and remade my bed. The sheets themselves were moist from the night air, but I did not say a word; I simply made the bed, undressed silently and slid between the damp sheets as she watched over me.

I received no treatment at all for my ankle, though by the following morning it had taken on a hideous bluish-purple hue and blown up like a large balloon. The only concession made to me was that I was kept in the house and schoolwork was brought over, but it would be many weeks before I could put even the slightest amount of weight on my ankle. I would pay for that untreated injury in the future, as by my early 20s I would have developed a number of joint and back problems as a direct result.

On some occasions, girls who had been at the approved school for a long time and who had behaved themselves were allowed home for a long weekend. With fewer girls to pick on, we soon became targets for Tanya and her gang, who had also had to stay behind, presumably because of the severity of their crimes. Each day became a losing battle as Mel and I were punched and kicked, with no one to protect us; plates of food would be knocked from our hands and we would have to go without a meal; and if Tanya or one of her gang said something had gone missing, the house mother would blame me without question. There seemed no limit to their spiteful cruelty. On the Sunday morning, as Mel and I fulfilled our breakfast duties, my friend poured the teas while I served the food. When Mel reached Tanya's table, the head girl complained the tea tasted disgusting and threw the contents of her scalding hot cup in Mel's face. Mel screamed in agony, but our house mother, who had witnessed it all, said nothing to Tanya, yet scolded us for making a mess and ordered us to make more tea. Out in the kitchen, Mel was still crying, and I could see how sore her face, neck and chest were as they were a bright red colour. She received no treatment for her burns, though, and the matter was never mentioned again.

The intense bullying at Tanya's hands petered out once the rest of the girls had returned, but when the next long weekend loomed, those who'd previously been the head girl's victims all knew what lay in store. During this weekend, the girls who'd been left behind were all grouped up into a couple of the other houses, and a new girl who'd been sent to the school just a few weeks earlier was transferred to our house. I'd only seen her in lessons up until this point, but she was a shy girl and just the type Tanya and her mob were sure to prey on. My fears proved to be true during her first day in our house, as the head girl would not leave her alone, bullying her mercilessly at every opportunity. However, nothing could have prepared her for what was to happen next.

That night, as we lay in our beds awaiting lights out, Tanya struck. Backed up by her gang members, she sauntered over to the new girl's bed and told her she had to be initiated into the group and the only way to do this was to prove herself to be one of them. Then Tanya turned to the other few of us who were not part of her gang and warned us in no uncertain terms we would be next if we did not join in what was about to follow. The poor girl cowered under her bedsheets with just her face exposed, staring wide-eyed at her tormentor, but this only served to spur Tanya on. With a glint in her eyes, she produced a hairbrush, brandishing the stiff bristles in her victim's face, and in a sudden flurry the gang grabbed her, stuffing socks into her mouth to silence the forthcoming screams. To my eternal shame, I too was part of this mob, so scared for my own safety that I was not prepared to take on the chief bully in case I would be next. Tanya wrenched back the bedsheets and with the stiff bristle end proceeded to rape her victim. She was then followed by her closest gang members, who prolonged the torture in the same fashion. Once they'd tired of that game, they forced the girl to masturbate with a drinks bottle. To this day, I can still vividly recall the poor girl's eyes as they bore into mine, silently pleading with me to help her as she suffered. I didn't have the courage, as I knew for certain that the same punishment would be mine if I challenged the head girl's authority, and I hated myself like never before for my cowardice.

Finally the pack departed, leaving their prey sobbing and bleeding on her bed, and it was only then I realised that the door to the room had been partly open the whole time. There in the shadows stood the bulky frame of our house mother, who must have witnessed the entire assault in all its depravity. She had had the power to prevent it happening or to stop it at any point, but she had let it run its entire sadistic course. That night I vowed to myself that I would leave this place and never come back or I would die trying.

A few days later, as Mel and I chatted, I expanded upon my escape plan, and the idea appealed to her as much as it did to me; what's more, Mel came from London and knew her way around, so she assured me if we could just make it to the city and lose ourselves there, we had every chance of never being caught, as she knew of someone she was sure would be willing to help us.

The escape plot itself seemed so simple, but even as youngsters we appreciated that simplicity was sometimes the best way forward. One Saturday a month, a group of girls deemed well enough behaved during the preceding weeks earned the privilege of a supervised trip to the local cinema, and Mel and I were determined we would be included in the next group, which was due to go into town the following weekend. Whatever provocation we faced during the next seven days we took with a smile; our joint rota service at mealtimes was of the highest order, and I even tried my best with my school assignments. Sure enough, come Saturday we were picked to be part of the lucky bunch to enjoy an afternoon out.

Mel and I had reason to be slightly more excited than the rest of the girls who were escorted by two house mothers to the cinema for the matinee performance, and our eyes darted furtively from left to right as we walked along, searching for the ideal spot to break away from the group on our way back to the institution. With a slight nod of heads towards each other, we knew we'd both spotted it.

Inside the cinema, the film we'd come to watch was a mere drone, and the minutes dragged their heels like a reluctant child. For Mel and me, the real excitement grew as we made our way out onto the main road and began the long walk home. Suddenly, at the point in the road we'd silently agreed upon, we were off, running as if our lives depended on it. We didn't look back as we weaved our way through parked cars in an area behind a row of shops. If we could just make it over the wall that stood between us and the field behind, we knew we would be home and dry, for even if the house mothers had been willing to leave the rest of the group unsupervised, they would never have made it over this high obstacle. I helped propel Mel to the top of the wall, and it seemed as if my arm would come out of its socket as she hoisted me skyward, but when we landed in the field on the other side, we allowed ourselves a brief smile as we tried to regain our breath.

After my previously failed escape bid, I knew we had to keep going, but I could feel a painful stitch building up in my side as Mel sprinted ahead of me towards a small coppice. Here, we stopped for a few moments to catch our breath before carrying on, hugging the edges of the field in the hope we would not been seen. By the time we reached the outskirts of a housing estate, I felt as if my lungs were fit to burst. What with it being a Saturday, there were still plenty of people about and children playing in the street, but despite our distinctive approved-school uniforms, nobody seemed to be paying us much attention, which was a rather amazing stroke of luck. Mel and I made for a playground and hung around the swings and slides until the evening drew in, laughing at our newfound freedom but still wary that it might be curtailed at any moment. As planned, we then made our way towards the main road but still kept a watchful eye out for any passing police cars. Luck seemed to be on our side, though, and as we spotted the first signs towards London, we knew we were on our way.

TEN

The Price of Admission

It seemed like the answer to our prayers when the car pulled up alongside us and a kind-looking old man leant across his passenger seat, wound down his window and offered us a lift. Mel and I had been walking for hours, and the muscles in the back of my legs ached with every step. London lay many miles away still, but when we told him our destination, he cheerily said he'd be happy to take us. We climbed into the back seat, and as we sank into the soft leather upholstery, it felt so good to rest our tired bodies. After we set off, the man asked us if we'd like a drink and a bite to eat. The mere mention of food reminded us we hadn't eaten for hours, so we were both happy to accept the invitation of a meal at his house before resuming our journey.

On entering his small house, it wasn't so much the front room's orange-yellowy wallpaper with its flowery circled pattern that struck me first but the stale musty smell which wafted throughout. However, beggars can't be choosers and, having accepted his hospitality, we gratefully sat down on the threadbare sofa as he lit the fire and went to the kitchen to make us some food. The man's jolly humming from the kitchen comforted us, and every now and again he popped his head around the door just to make sure we were all right. Mel and I were too tired to talk to each other, but we both felt calm and relaxed; it was as if we'd both come to the same conclusion that this old man, who had the demeanour of a kindly granddad, was probably lonely and grateful for our company. Eventually, he returned from the kitchen with a plate of sandwiches and steaming mugs of tomato soup. The smell made my mouth water, and along with the fire's warm glow the soup worked wonders in warming us up after our long walk in the chilly night air.

It was getting quite late by now, and the man suggested that, because we both looked so tired, it might be better if we stayed the night and he drove us to London in the morning. We'd feel better after a good night's sleep, he said. As he departed with the tray, we decided to accept his kind offer, mostly because it was very late and there was far more chance of two teenagers out after dark getting picked up by the police. We told him our decision when he returned from the kitchen, and he seemed genuinely pleased, as if we were doing him a favour.

The man went through to another room and came back with an armful of pillows and blankets for us to make a bed up on the floor, and as we set about doing this he disappeared again, this time returning with a bundle of clothes. It was as if he couldn't do enough to help us, so it came as a bit of a shock when he next said, 'You've run away, haven't you?'

Mel and I exchanged nervous glances, but he assured us he was not going to tell anyone and that we could trust him. He'd certainly given us no reason not to so far. To break the silence, he threw the clothes on the floor and said we'd be better off changing out of our approved-school uniforms, as the police would surely have a description of us. He'd also given us a shirt each to sleep in, and with that he went to bed, leaving Mel and me alone. There was certainly nothing in this nice old man's behaviour to arouse our suspicions.

The sound of the door opening woke me from my slumber: a situation I'd experienced too many times before. I became aware that the man was climbing into the makeshift bed on Mel's side, and I suddenly felt her shove him away as she exclaimed, 'No!' The flickering firelight threw frantic shadows across the room as he grabbed my friend's hands and held them down on either side of her head. I scrambled up in a vain attempt to stop him but, with a twisted smile I found all too familiar, he looked me directly in the eyes and said, 'Nothing's for free', before threatening to inform the police if we did not comply with his demands. I glared at him and he held my stare before Mel stopped struggling and I turned over to face the other way. All I could hear were Mel's sobs and his grunts and moans as I lay there rigid and silent, waiting for him to finish, knowing deep down it would be my turn next.

He fell silent for a while, but just as it seemed I might be spared I felt his hands start to slide over my body. I gagged at the rancid, sour odour which emanated from his body as it reminded me so much of Ronald, but I didn't say anything and I didn't struggle; I just willed it to be over as quickly as possible. As I lay there under him, I traced the wallpaper's intricate pattern in the dimming firelight and tried to float away to the safe place in my mind where I could see myself dancing, spinning and floating in my beautiful dress as the turntable at the London Palladium spun around and around.

With a grunt, he rolled off me and, without so much as a word to either of us, left the room. Mel was sobbing her heart out and we clung together in silence; there were no words we could say to soothe each other. 'Nothing's for free,' he'd said, and in that moment we both realised that in our case he was right. Everything has its price and for us our bodies were the only currency we had with which to pay. Over the next few months, we would make similar transactions time and time again, and it came to mean nothing more than simply taking money out of a purse and handing it over in return for the goods we needed. During payment, 'we' were never there, only our bodies, like lumps of meat on a slab, so I held Mel tight as she cried but shed no tears of my own – I already knew there wasn't any point.

The following morning, this rapist pensioner entered the front room with a cheery smile and started humming in his tuneless manner as he made us breakfast, for, as he said, he couldn't let us go on our way with empty stomachs. We dressed in the clothes he'd given us the night before and left in his car, Mel and I gazing silently out of our side windows until we reached the outskirts of London, where he dropped us off with a friendly wave. My friend and I didn't speak of the night before as we spent the rest of the day making our way over to London's East End, where Mel knew a man named

Brian, whom she said would put us up. We walked until it seemed we would drop, but finally that evening we reached a little two-up two-down terraced house on a road bisected by a railway line. Brian's house was the last one before the viaduct that rumbled regularly with each passing train. As we approached the front door, I hoped desperately he'd be there and wouldn't turn us away.

A painter and decorator by trade, Brian spent a lot of time away from home, living in digs as he moved from one job to the next, and he often let acquaintances doss down on his floor for the odd night or two. I don't know how Mel knew him, but he didn't seem too perturbed when we turned up on his doorstep, explained we were on the run and needed a place to stay. He readily agreed we could stay for a few days before we found somewhere else, but I was in for quite a shock once we'd stepped over the threshold. The downstairs was a heaving mess of junk, and I soon learnt that Brian used only the upstairs as living quarters. There was a first-floor front sitting room with two sash windows, a back bedroom and a small kitchenette to the side. As he was away from home so much, it appeared Brian had neither the time nor the inclination to sort out the mess downstairs, which meant you had literally to squeeze your way through the back room to get to the outside toilet. The toilet itself was just a very small dark hut full of cobwebs and with newspaper squares hung up on a nail, but I was not complaining. It may not have been the nicest of places, but at least it offered some privacy; there was no house mother standing over you as you tried to pee. With no bathroom to speak of, Mel and I would strip and wash in the upstairs sink, and we slept on the floor using Brian's old coats as blankets, huddling close in order to stay warm.

For our first two days, Brian was away working, so Mel and I survived on a stale loaf of bread we'd found in the kitchen. We discovered if we toasted the slices it was far easier to pick off the mould; it also felt better to have something warm inside us and, with nothing else on offer, needs must. Needs also dictated that we really couldn't lose this roof over our heads, so Mel and I decided to clear up the house as best we could and do Brian's washing whilst he was away, in the hope he'd let us stay on longer than the couple of days agreed. We beavered away with all our might, shifting boxes and crates out of the way to create a bit of space downstairs and hand washing Brian's clothes in the sink by scrubbing a block of soap into them. Our efforts paid dividends, as when he returned he was so pleased with us he decide to strike a deal: we kept house for him – and his bed warm when he wanted it – and in return we could stay as long as we needed to. It didn't take long to weigh up the pros and cons: if it meant not going back to the approved school, then it was worth it. Everyone got what he or she wanted.

Too scared to venture outside in the first few weeks, we spent much of the time gazing out of the front first-floor windows at the carriages which passed by on the viaduct, and the rumble of each oncoming train brought with it a peculiar comfort and pain. I enjoyed spotting the faces of the commuters, but it was all too easy to envy them, wishing I had a home and a family and a normal life to return to, whatever that might be.

Brian did give us a small amount of money on occasion and, driven by hunger, we would make a quick dash to the shops to pick up bread, soup and baked beans before scurrying back to our bolt-hole, but with the spectre looming over us of being caught by the police, such trips were not something to look forward to. It was only later we had the courage to go to a café and work our way through plates of eggs, bacon, sausages, beans and tomatoes all washed down with large mugs of tea, and these were such special days. Our only other source of food was from the many and varied transient inhabitants who shared the floor we slept on for a day or two before moving on. These men brought bottles of beer and bags of chips with them, and in exchange for giving them what they wanted, we would eat well for the evening. Some were nice and some not so nice, but no one knocked us around, and it didn't really matter if we liked them or not as it was just a simple exchange of goods.

Mel and I both smoked, but we had no money for luxuries like cigarettes, so apart from scrounging what we could from those passing through, the only other reason we would step outside the front door was to pick up dog-ends in the street, then rush back and empty their contents into a small tin. A dock leaf placed on top served to keep the old tobacco moist enough, and from this we would roll our own extremely thin cigarettes, careful not to waste so much as a strand of the precious tobacco. We became quite inventive with our clothes, too, for as the warmer months approached, we needed something more appropriate. By altering some of Brian's old clothes we managed to create a whole new wardrobe, albeit a slightly hippyish-looking one.

Mel and I got on really well during these months, and the approved school was gradually becoming a dim and distant memory. However, it's only natural to need other company, and as we watched the men playing kick-about in the street as the weather improved, we both longed to call down for a chat. But we couldn't take the chance of drawing attention to ourselves.

Eventually, however, temptation got the better of us, and we called down to the men below. I soon struck up a friendship with one called Keith, a quiet and gentle man who made me melt when he said nice things to me. He was married with three children, but this didn't mean anything to me, and after a while our relationship grew. I never told him my real age, and we slept together a few times, but it was wholly different than with the other men, as it never felt like he was using me.

When summer came, Mel and I began sneaking out to the heath at Whipps Cross, where we could lie down in the long grass and sunbathe without fear of being seen from the road or by passers-by. We'd spend hours chatting about fashion or music and singing songs we'd heard on Brian's radio, such as Mungo Jerry's 'In The Summertime', a song that can still stop me in my tracks to this day. On other occasions, we'd steal make-up and return to the house to experiment on each other. In some respects, we were therefore no different from any other teenagers. Mel was my first really close friend, and though we never spoke about our pasts or the approved school, our joint experiences bonded us together in a way that couldn't be expressed in words.

Mel proved her loyalty to me when I found out that I'd fallen pregnant. Ridiculous though it may sound, I hadn't fully understood that this could happen as a result of what I'd been doing with Keith and the other men, but Mel was better informed than me and explained what was going on when my periods stopped and my stomach started to grow. I knew in my heart of hearts the father was Keith, but I was terrified. Mel was as supportive as any friend could be, promising to find a job so she could look after both me and the baby. I think we both knew it was unrealistic, but it was a comforting dream which kept us both going.

ELEVEN

Someone to Watch Over Me

Drifting back into consciousness, I suddenly woke with a terrible start. As my eyes cleared, I didn't recognise the room or the four or five dark faces staring down at me. I struggled to move, but my hands were tied above my head and both of my legs were being held down in a vice-like grip. Between my legs lay another man, inside of me, hurting me. Having grunted his satisfaction, he wiped me down with a white handkerchief before stuffing it in my mouth as another man took his place and the prolonged ordeal resumed. It was at that point I passed out again, for this was no dream; it was a living nightmare.

When the knock at the door came that led to this hell, Brian had been away on a job, and Mel and I were petrified the police had finally found us. Gingerly, we pulled a gap in the curtain and, to our relief, the three black men standing at the door were not in uniform. One was a big man, not fat but very tall and powerfully built; a skinny man wearing a bright purple paisley shirt stood to one side of him and a short stumpy man in a suit smoking a cigar to the other, the sunlight bouncing off the latter's many rings each time he took the cigar from his mouth. I opened the window to ask them what they wanted and the stumpy man replied that they were looking for Brian. He seemed genuinely disappointed when I went downstairs to open the front door and told him Brian was away, for by all accounts they had arranged to meet for a drink and something to eat. I noticed the big tall guy had taken a step or two back from the others and had an air of agitation about him as if he needed to be somewhere, but apart from this there was nothing to set my alarm bells ringing. The stumpy little man offered to take Mel and me out for a drink and some fish and chips and, having lived off nothing but stale bread for the past week or so, the thought of such a feast made our mouths water. I looked at Mel and we came to a silent agreement; the men seemed nice enough, and even if they wanted paying in the customary manner at the end of the night, it would be worth it, wouldn't it?

The daylight drifted into dusk as we sat outside the pub, happily eating fish and chips and drinking beer. Our companions had been friendly enough, so we didn't hesitate when the stumpy one offered us a lift home. I climbed into the back of his car and must have passed out immediately, as the next thing I remember is awakening after the gang rape had begun.

In the darkened room, I was intermittently aware of the tall man sitting across the way and staring at me as I drifted in and out of consciousness. I struggled to catch a glimpse of Mel, but she was nowhere to be seen, and

I panicked as I spotted the stumpy man enter the room. He forced a handful of pills into my mouth, holding it shut until I'd swallowed them. I had no strength to fight back and the lead weight of my body lay slumped. Time seemed to flow unchecked as more faces hovered above me, men laughing, then more pills were pumped into me. Somewhere in my mind I was sure I had seen Mel slumped naked on the floor – at least, I thought it was her.

Someone tried to give me food and water, but I was so sleepy I couldn't stay awake to take it. Next, someone was shaking me and slapping my face before the shock of ice-cold water drenched me. Gradually, the mushy haze subsided, and I could indeed see Mel in the corner with a blanket thrown over her and blood dripping from her puffy lip. I looked down and saw that I too was covered in a blanket; underneath I was naked. Slowly but surely the pinpricks of pain spread all over my sore and tender body as I watched the stumpy man talk to the other two from the pub. I couldn't make out what was being said and, as my mind clicked back into gear, I was filled with terror at the prospect of what might happen to us next.

What seemed like hours slipped by as Mel and I sat on the floor, and I began to take in my surroundings. We were trapped in a large double-bay-fronted room with high ceilings, the paper was peeling from the walls and there was no furniture apart from a sofa, a couple of chairs and a low coffee table. Bottles of beer and empty or part-empty vodka bottles covered the table, while the floor was hidden beneath empty takeaway cartons, scraps of spilt food and ashtrays overflowing with cigarette butts. The only exit was the one door, and there would be no escape from here.

Darkness had fallen on the second day when we were ordered to get ourselves cleaned up and dressed, as we were leaving. The tall man escorted us to the bathroom upstairs, where we did our best to wash and put our clothes back on. All three men were waiting for us when we came out of the bathroom, and we were quickly bundled into the car outside, too dazed and confused to scream for help in the street. We drove in silence for a good 15 minutes before the car pulled up outside another house and we were pushed in through the door. Once we were inside, the stumpy man wasted no time in forcing more tablets down my throat, but I gagged and only the intervention of the tall man saved me from another beating. I swallowed down the tablets, terrified about what was to come. 'Please don't hurt me,' I pleaded. 'I'm pregnant, please don't hurt my baby.'

The two shorter men laughed in my face, and I was hauled into another room with a bed in the middle. I was pushed down and once again my hands were tied behind my head. From the other room, I could hear Mel desperately calling out my name, and on hearing her cries, I lashed out, trying to struggle free as I kicked with my legs. My resistance was futile; the skinny man started punching me before grabbing me around the throat. I glimpsed the light from the naked bulb glancing off his glasses before slipping down through what felt like a black hole and then nothing.

As before, I slipped in and out of consciousness, and I was no longer sure of anything apart from the faces above me, laughing and jeering as I was pulled

around like a rag doll for their pleasure. I caught a
fleeting glimpse of Mel being knocked from one side
of the room to the other. More pills were pushed down
my throat, and in my lucid moments it seemed as if the
violence was getting worse. Over and over, I could hear
my muffled disembodied voice from far away pleading,
'Please don't hurt my baby.'

Time became increasingly difficult to judge, but we
spent at least two days at this second address, during
which time a fight broke out between the tall man and
the stumpy one when the tall one stopped him punching
me. The pills and the beatings continued until it was
decided we should be moved again, but this time on
foot, with Mel and me sandwiched between the two
smaller men at the front and the tall man at the back.
'Run,' whispered the tall man as we reached an area
with a road running adjacent to us. 'Run,' he urged us
again and, turning around sharply to look at him, we
could vaguely make out the direction he was pointing
through the pitch black of the night. With a stumbling
gait, caused by our drugged states, we fled our assailants
as fast as we could, and eventually the sounds of them
fighting and shouting amongst themselves faded into
the distance.

Finally, we could run no more, and we wandered
around for ages in an area we didn't recognise, half
expecting to come face to face with our attackers at
any moment. More by luck than judgement, Mel and I
found ourselves in an area of east London from which
she knew the way back to Brian's house. The house
was in darkness when we arrived, so we retrieved the
spare key from under a flowerpot and stumbled through

the front door, exhausted, battered and bruised. But there was no time to check our wounds; first we had to barricade the door in case they came back for us, as this house was no longer the safe haven it had been. Then we went upstairs to the kitchen at the back, where we sat huddled together, slumped over the table until sleep finally came to take us away from this crazy nightmare.

When the early morning sun lit the kitchen and woke us, we were stiff and sore with a thirst it seemed no amount of water could quench for days after. I tended to Mel's cuts and she cleaned mine as we took turns washing in the kitchen sink. We were so bruised, cut and swollen down below, all we could do was fill the sink with warm water and take turns to sit our bottoms in it, dangling our legs over the side as we tried to soothe the pain a little. Neither of us had any idea what day of the week it was or for how long we'd been held captive, but we guessed we'd been away for at least four, if not five, days.

Mel and I could not bring ourselves to talk about what had happened: it was just too hard to cope with. After all, we had accepted the invitation for a meal and a drink, so in our minds we deserved what had happened: it was all our fault. Going to the police was obviously not an option, as we were still on the run, so we told no one and simply swallowed the whole episode down with the rest of the pain. I would be well into my 40s before I could even admit to myself that I was gang-raped and it was not my fault. The deep-seated memories were always there, but they always seemed just out of reach in my mind, almost like a black-and-white old-fashioned movie playing distantly in the background. Some clips were clear and some grainy to the point of being non-existent, but I was always aware on some level that the clip was still there.

When Brian returned, life continued as what passed for normal. Mel and I did mention that three black men had come around asking for him, but this confused Brian as he had not made any arrangements to go out and did not have any black friends. We began to realise that the three men must have been watching Brian's house for some time and known we were alone. When the opportunity arose, they grabbed us and sold us for group sex, keeping us drugged all the while so we did not cause any trouble. What struck fear into my heart was the growing belief that if the tall man had not finally taken pity on us and helped us to escape, we would not have survived, as the violence had been growing worse. All I had to be thankful for was that at three months' pregnant I had not lost my baby, for somehow we had both survived this ordeal.

Through Brian's connections, he knew how to get hold of fake IDs, and he now promised that for the usual price one would be mine. It seemed the ideal solution, as I had to find a way to ensure I never had to go back to my birth-parents if I managed to evade the police. An ID would give me the chance to get a job and earn the money necessary to look after my baby, and Mel said she would help me by working after the baby was born. However, an even more off-beat opportunity was about to present itself in the shape of Ian, a friend of Brian's who came by the house from time to time. He knew I was pregnant and also knew about my plans to use a fake ID to secure employment. When he suggested instead that we got married as a way of ensuring that no one would find me, I didn't know what to say at first. I somehow doubt he would have made such a proposal if he'd known I was only 14 years old at the time. Nevertheless, using my fake ID, a farcical marriage of sorts took place at the local church and, in my immaturity, not only did I now feel safe, I was also excited about the fact that I would now have a family of my own. All I had ever wanted was to feel that I belonged somewhere, and at first I thought this was my chance.

The marriage marked the end of an era for Mel and me. I was to move in with Ian, and my friend made plans to return to her parents in the hope that they might be able to persuade the authorities to allow her to stay. She promised me faithfully she would not under any circumstances tell anyone where I was and, on parting, we hugged each other and cried, then hugged each other again, promising to keep in touch but somehow knowing this would never happen. We had been through so much together, suffering a gang rape that would subconsciously affect my life at every turn for many years to come and must surely have had the same effect on Mel, yet now we were going our separate ways, never to meet again.

I still saw Keith from time to time, and he seemed as certain as I was that the baby I was carrying was his. He told me in these brief moments that he wanted to leave his wife and get away from his overbearing mother-in-law, who lived next door, just so he could be with me, but my husband happened to overhear one of these conversations and a dreadful argument ensued. Ian stated he'd married me to protect me and he neither needed nor wanted Keith hanging around. As far as he was concerned, he would be the child's father and that was the end of the matter.

Even after this argument, Keith still came to see me as regularly as he could without Ian's knowledge. Married life with Ian hadn't turned out the way I'd hoped, and whenever I was with this kind man I felt as though I was really in love, although being so young I was perhaps more in love with the idea of being in love. Matters eventually came to a head on the evening Keith came around to the digs I shared with Ian to tell him that he was going to leave his wife and wanted to be with me. Another argument broke out as Ian sensed he was losing what he thought was his and finally he stormed out, leaving Keith and me together. That night we lay in each other's arms discussing the forthcoming birth of our baby and what life together would be like. In that moment, I truly believed no one would hurt me again because I was now protected by Keith's love.

A sharp insistent knocking at the front door woke us very early the following morning, and when Keith finally answered it, there stood two police officers. After the confrontation, my phoney husband had contacted the authorities to inform them where they could find a runaway.

TWELVE

A Babe in Arms

As I lay in my hospital bed and gazed at the four walls of the small room, I tried to make sense of the previous 24 hours. The police interview had been mercifully short, perhaps due to my one-word answers and determination not to tell the officers anything that could connect me to Brian. I didn't give them any details about how we had lived our lives since running away, and I certainly never mentioned the gang rape, as at that point I still placed the blame firmly at my own feet. However, the arrest had unnerved me. I was genuinely terrified I would be sent back to the approved school, my baby would be taken from me and I would be trapped once more in the life I had tried to escape.

I'd been referred to hospital after a medical check at the police station. I was having extremely painful stomach cramps and was covered in a rash. My health was pretty poor in general, but I suppose this was only to be expected after months of living in the squat and surviving on a very inadequate diet. I had numerous examinations, which was just as well considering I was by now six months pregnant and this was my first check-up. As I pondered my predicament, I heard the door handle being turned, but instead of a nurse coming in to check on me as I'd expected, there stood my mum. She came over to sit on my bed and took me in her arms without a word. This simple gesture of comfort caused me to cry with such fury I thought the tears would choke me.

Mum explained that I'd been in all the papers during the initial days of the police search and, as she held me, she softly asked if anyone had hurt me. For the first time since my ordeal, I managed to put into words something of what had happened to me at the hands of the gang who had abducted Mel and me that night. I thought she was going to hug me and tell me it was going to be all right, as she always had when I was little and had fallen over and hurt myself or had had a fight with my brother but, instead of wiping away my tears, I felt her stiffen and pull away from me. All she could say was 'Oh dear.' Perhaps my opening up in this way was too painful for her, but nothing more was said about the matter, and it would not be raised between us again for nearly 40 years. She then admitted that she found it all too hard to deal with and simply didn't know what to say or do when I'd told her. I know now this wasn't her fault, but back then, though I knew she loved me, it became one of those episodes when my love for her was punctuated by feelings of resentment and abandonment that were left hanging in the air between us.

To my utter relief, I was informed I was not to be sent back to the approved school but to a mother-and-baby home, and within hours of arriving there, I felt settled and calm. The staff were pleasant and kind, and for the first time in years, I felt free from the constant threat of violence hanging over me. My health took a while to improve, but at least I was eating properly again. When I attended the antenatal appointments at the hospital, the medics didn't seem overly concerned that my unborn baby was rather small for that stage of the pregnancy, and everything seemed to be proceeding normally. I spent my days making blankets and stuffed toys in happy expectation as I waited for my baby's arrival. I couldn't remember ever feeling quite so happy. However, no one ever accompanied me on my trips to the hospital, and I couldn't help feeling there was a sense of shame connected to my unborn child. There was still a stigma attached to unmarried mothers in the 1970s, and I always felt there was great emphasis placed on the word 'Miss' whenever I was called from the waiting room.

Although the standard of care at the home couldn't be questioned, no one there talked to any of the girls about what giving birth would actually be like. I therefore had no idea what to expect, but on the morning of 3 April 1971, I was about to find out. Having gone into labour, I was rushed into hospital, and I was so frightened I kept crying for my mum. For the most part I was left alone in a room, and I found if I got up and walked around the pain seemed to ease a bit. However, each time a nurse came in and caught me, I'd be told off and made to lie down again. There was one nurse, however, who seemed to fully appreciate how isolated and scared I felt, and she made every effort to be with me whenever she could. At the end, she told me to squeeze her hand as tightly as I wanted, and the following day

I had to apologise when she showed me the fingernail marks I'd left in her hand. By then I had given birth to my beautiful daughter: a small baby with a mop of thick dark hair, which confirmed to me she was Keith's daughter, and perfect in every way. I loved her so very much from the moment I first saw her.

I only had one set of visitors while I remained in hospital, and I couldn't have been more surprised when Ronald and Emily entered the room. Emily even brought a matinee jacket with matching bootees and mittens she'd made herself, and all the talk was of how I should now come home, that things would be different and they really needed me. They didn't ask me about where I had been, how I had fallen pregnant or who the father of my baby was. It seemed that this was all to be swept under the carpet. I noticed, however, that Ronald never once even so much as looked at his granddaughter, and when I declined their invitation to return, his manner changed in an instant. He told me that if I was a good daughter I would come back, but that I was too wicked and selfish. Thankfully, that was their only visit to the hospital, as by the time they'd finally left I felt confused, tired and emotional. But with just one look at my beautiful little girl my overwhelming sense of joy returned, and I would lie for hours just staring at her peacefully sleeping. I felt so lucky to have someone in my life to love who was mine and who would love me, too. At long last I had my own family, and no one would ever take her away from me.

On returning to the home, I found it difficult at first to comply with the rule that the babies were kept in a communal nursery during the day and we mothers were only allowed to see them at feeding times, when we would also change them. For the rest of the day, the matron on duty would watch over them. It wasn't until night-time that we were reunited with our babies and could take them upstairs with us to sleep in cots by our beds.

I will never forget the sense of pride I felt when Mum and Dad came to visit and I could show off my daughter, whom I had called Heidi. To me, it felt like I had a chance to prove that I could be good at something. I would be the best mother that I could be and somehow that would erase all the other mistakes I had made. I would make them proud of me.

The home was never meant to be permanent accommodation. Mothers and their new babies were only allowed to stay for up to six weeks after giving birth, at which point either the baby was given up for adoption or mother and child were found a new place to stay. Social services soon began applying pressure for me to give up Heidi. Not only was I just 15 years old, which barred me from living on my own, but having turned down my birth-parents there was nowhere else I could stay. Their arguments might have seemed logical, but my mind was already set: Heidi and I would remain together no matter what. Everything good I'd ever had had been taken from me, but not this time. Eventually the authorities conceded and a place was found for me at a Catholic mother-and-baby home about five miles away.

The house itself was a huge old property, and on my first day, I was led upstairs to a large room at the front with a big bay window that let in plenty of light. The fixtures and fittings consisted of a bed, a cot for the baby, fitted cupboards, a table and chairs and a sink, and my first impressions were that it really could feel like our own little home. There were perhaps seven other girls with their newborns living there, and if the weather was fine, all of the babies were snuggled into their prams and parked outside in the large garden. On wet-weather days, the tots would be left in their cots in our rooms, with one of the girls assigned the task of checking on them throughout the day. The rest of us had our own daily duties, whether this be cleaning the vast property, making everyone's meals for the day or growing vegetables and fruit in the garden and tending to the lawns and flower beds. There was always a great deal to be done, and we worked very hard from morning to night, sometimes even being taken to other people's gardens in the neighbourhood to tend their lawns. None of us complained, however, least of all me, as not only was I now safe, no one came to my bed at night and there were no more beatings.

My one concern, which was shared by the other girls, was that the staff were very strict about the contact we had with our children, which was restricted to first thing in the morning, mealtimes and last thing at night. Emily might not have possessed a mother's instinct to protect and nurture her child, but I did, and my heart ached at being parted for long hours from my baby girl. Often I would go up to feed her and find her crying her eyes out, a small red ball all hot and unhappy, and I found this unbearable, as I had no way of knowing how long she had been in discomfort. On one occasion, I even found her with her head wedged between the bars of her cot, and I was in a total panic as I struggled to free her and calm her down. However, my reaction was not to complain about my baby being neglected but to keep it a secret, as I was so scared that someone would take her away from me. It was already so deeply ingrained in me that all misfortune was ultimately my own fault. If I lost Heidi, I felt I would only have myself to blame.

As the home was a religious institution, great pressure was placed on the young mothers to have their babies christened. When Emily and Ronald began visiting me in the home, my birth-father was quick to pounce on this, insisting, as the son of a vicar, it was the right thing to do and that failure to comply would result in us both going to hell. I was wicked and might well be going anyway, but I did not want my daughter to suffer, so I agreed.

The day itself was beautiful, with all of the members of my family around me. Heidi's father was even allowed to attend, which was the first time I'd seen him since the police had caught up with me, as the authorities had not allowed us any contact since. After the service, we began writing to each other, and we would meet on the odd occasion I took Heidi shopping or to the clinic. When Keith held her in his arms, for a brief happy moment we were a family. I felt so elated, but I was still only a child playing at being an adult.

Ronald began repeating his request for me to come and live with him and Emily, assuring me everything would be better now. A similar pressure was being applied by social services, and the seed that Heidi and I could be part of a happy family had been well and truly sown in my mind. But it wasn't Ronald and Emily I wanted to live with, it was my parents. I longed for their Sunday afternoon visits, when we would go to Hampton Court or Windsor for the day to enjoy a family picnic, with Dad carrying Heidi on his hip for hours on end as we walked around the gardens and grounds. These were very special times for me, but I yearned to be with my parents permanently, and the fear that my request would be rejected hung over me like a cloud.

One evening I could not contain myself any longer, and my heart raced as I dialled the number to their shop. When Mum answered the phone, all I could do was blurt out my plea to be allowed to return to the shop to live with them. The seconds seemed like hours as I waited for her reply, but finally Mum replied that it just wasn't possible. Not only was there just not enough room for both my baby and me but also Uncle Harry would never allow it. An anger like I'd never known suddenly burst forth, and I screamed down the telephone, swearing at her wildly, which was the first and last time I've ever done so. Afterwards, I went back to my room, curled up with Heidi in my arms and sobbed into my pillow, despondent at the realisation that the only other option left open to me was to take Ronald up on his offer and return to my birth-parents' house. I tried to convince myself that perhaps things really could be different this time around. I was determined to be the good daughter they'd always wanted, and then they would love me at last.

Social services and my birth-parents were delighted by my change of heart, but on the day of my return it took all my strength to walk through the front door into that house. However, like a puppy that has been subdued by endless beatings, I returned to the fold and tried to push my reservations to the back of my mind. I carried Heidi to the upstairs room we would share together and unpacked our belongings, consoling myself with the thought that I would now be able to spend some quality time with my baby, who was already seven months old, for the first time since she was born.

Initially, all seemed quite bearable as life settled into a routine. I became Ronald's and Emily's eyes and ears once more, making phone calls for them and generally taking care of the house, but I had not accounted for one major adjustment I would have to make. For the past year, I had lived with a lot of girls who were not much older than me in the two different mother-and-baby homes, but now I had no friends or contact with any other mothers. My only communication was with Emily and Ronald. This led to a sense of isolation and loneliness I'd never previously felt with such intensity, and it soon began to take its toll. After another day cooking and cleaning for my birth-parents and attending to their needs, I would lie awake at night listening to the radio in bed while Heidi slept beside me. I was acutely aware she was the only source of true happiness in my life now, but in moments of brutal honesty I had to admit that, as much as I loved her, in other ways, on levels I couldn't explain, I felt somehow disconnected from her. Perhaps this was due to the times at the homes we had been kept apart when we should have been bonding; perhaps the staff believed most girls would eventually give their babies up for adoption so this was for the best. Whatever the reason,

I would often cry myself to sleep just wishing there was someone out there who would want both me and my daughter, someone who would talk to me, hold me and love me. The child in me still craved the fairytale ending, the 'happy ever after'. Looking back, I can see that, after all I had gone through, I wasn't emotionally mature enough to look after myself, never mind a baby, and it was almost as if I viewed Heidi as a doll that was mine to dress up and look after. In my case notes from that period, it is interesting to read my social worker's comments: 'Izzy dressed [Heidi] in a rather frilly dress and the outfit was completed with hat, mittens and boots – a rather doll-like effect. Izzy seems detached from the baby when she is handling her, often handles her casually, and while making the "right" cooing noises, these seem to have little relation to the baby's mood or needs.'

I was a damaged and mistrustful 15-year-old, and I was sick of other people telling me what to do. But this stubbornness was also mixed with feelings of inadequacy and fears that I would never be good enough, that I was a bad girl and had deserved everything that had happened to me up to that point. I desperately wanted to be loved and to belong somewhere, and it was this all-consuming need that would determine the course of our lives from now on.

One night, after putting Heidi to sleep in her cot, I decided to go for a bath, and in a moment of introspection these feelings and wishes flooded over me so suddenly I found myself sobbing uncontrollably, to the point that I lay there in the bath wishing once more I could go to sleep and never have to wake up again. Only the chilly air as I stepped from the bath seemed to shake me from my sombre mood and bring me to my senses, and I dried myself quickly and went to bed. Yet that same night I found myself doing something I had never dreamed possible. As I lay there, I longed for Ronald to come to my bed as he used to, anything just so long as I could feel the closeness of another human being. These thoughts became a recurring theme after that night, exciting me in a way that made me feel disgusted with myself. I felt sick to the core, but I could not erase these feelings, and they in turn revived the guilt of my being wicked and evil. Surely I was, I had to be, to want my own father to come to my bed?

Mum and Dad did come to visit me a couple of times, but whilst I tried not to let it show, my resentment at having been abandoned by them again, as I saw it, made me feel very distant from them. I certainly never took these opportunities to get my feelings out in the open; we simply made small talk and I built my 'protective wall' around me just that little bit higher. However, I would soon come to realise I was cutting off my nose to spite my face.

Ronald had always had a volatile nature, but as time passed his moods seemed to be getting much worse, even more unpredictable and intense than I remembered them being as a small child. One afternoon, while I was playing out in the garden with Heidi, the relative quiet was suddenly shattered by Emily's shouts. I could also hear Ronald raging at her, and the noise appeared to be coming from the upstairs toilet. I quickly made Heidi comfortable then darted inside, taking the stairs two at a time, only to find my birth-father trying to drag his wife out of the toilet by her hair. Having successfully evicted Emily from the bathroom by force, Ronald slammed the door shut and locked himself in. I took my birth-mother downstairs and, once she was sufficiently calm, she explained the row had started because she was in the toilet at the same time he had wanted to use it. He was not a man to be told to wait in his own house. Such fights became more and more common, and I began to feel so sorry for Emily as it seemed she had become the person at whom he directed all his venomous anger and hatred.

Despite his long history of violence and abuse, it truly hadn't occurred to me up until this point that perhaps my daughter might also be in danger from him. I'd always assumed that because I was so wicked I was the only victim he ever vented his frustrations on, but it had become clear to me this wasn't the case. What if Heidi, who was now nearly a year old, got in his way when he was in a foul mood – worse still, what if he started to touch her in the way he had me? I knew there and then I had to leave; there was no way I could live under the same roof as my birth-parents. I'd just turned 16 and was now eligible for work, so, without telling my birth-parents, I visited the labour exchange in search of a means to escape. I was told I could move into a hostel and someone would look after Heidi whilst I was out at work, but I couldn't bear the thought of being separated from her for long hours again, so it was suggested I look for employment as a live-in housekeeper. I returned home that evening armed with a copy of *The Lady* magazine, laid Heidi down on her cot and secretly scoured the job ads in search of a position.

THIRTEEN

Love and Marriage?

It never even occurred to me that I might not be capable of doing the job; after all, I'd been running an entire household since the age of seven and my life experiences were pretty comprehensive for someone of my age. But with so much riding on me getting this position, I took a second to compose myself before walking up the drive of the smart house of my prospective new employer.

I'd seen the magazine advert for a live-in housekeeper to a man with two young girls a couple of weeks before and decided to apply, but after the 30-minute bus ride to his home, I suddenly suffered pre-interview butterflies. However, Mr Harrison, a man in his 30s whose wife had gone off with someone else and left their children with their father, couldn't have been nicer on our first meeting, during which I was also introduced to his daughters. By the end of the interview, Steve, as he'd asked me to call him, had given me a complete tour of the house, explained what my duties would be and offered me the job. I could barely contain my excitement. The pay wasn't particularly good, but the position came with room and board, and I could keep my daughter with me, which was all that really mattered.

The only snags I could see were, first, that I had to gain my social worker's permission, as I would remain a ward of court for another 12 months; then, more significantly, I also had to inform my birth-parents I was moving out. Ronald could not control his anger at the news, and during the meeting with the social worker, he made up some tale that I had tried to attack him again with the iron. This was ridiculous, as I would never have dared to do something of this kind. At the conclusion to this particularly fraught meeting, I sighed with relief when the social worker decided it might be a good idea for me to take up the position, pending a meeting with Mr Harrison and an inspection of the living quarters in which my daughter and I would stay. It was a mere formality, and in no time my bags were packed and I was ready to start my new life. Reading back through my notes, however, I can see that there were concerns, my social worker writing: 'I have my doubts about it to say the least . . . [I] see potential difficulties — especially the collusion of fantasy that must to some extent arise.'

My fantasy, of course, was that I would become part of the family. My job was to clean the house, cook and wash, take the girls to school and playschool and then pick them up again. Their mother only came to see them every other weekend, so we soon became quite attached to one another. I was very proud of my ability to keep house, and my employer was always full of praise for me, which made me feel needed and appreciated. Ronald had never thanked or complimented me, nothing I'd ever done had been good enough for him, so I finally felt like I was doing something right and couldn't have been happier.

Steve travelled a lot with his work, but we still managed to spend a lot of time together and went on outings such as swimming trips and even a holiday in a caravan. One night while we were away and I had put the children to bed, Steve put his arm around me as we sat together, and when he made to kiss me, I didn't object. Following that, we were soon enjoying a full relationship and, after what can only be described as a whirlwind romance, I said yes to him without hesitation when he asked me to marry him, my earlier illegal marriage to Ian having been annulled. In my mind, I'd found someone who both loved and valued me. He was a good father and seemed to adore Heidi, including her in all the treats for his two girls. He was a hard worker who was committed to looking after his family. He offered the stability that I craved and, at long last, it seemed that my fantasy was going to come true.

Due to my age, we had to ask social services for their permission, but they happily agreed, and I suspected they were pleased to have me off their books. Once again, my case notes offer a slightly different picture, my social worker commenting that: 'Insofar as I am in a position to give consent, I do not raise any objection to the marriage . . . We understand that [Miss Baird] is likely to proceed to get married whatever we decide and all we can hope is that she does so with the fullest awareness of the possible implications.' I later learnt that while my family had strong reservations, they were also of the opinion that there was little point in trying to change my mind.

The ceremony itself was booked at the local register office, and as the day approached, I was really looking forward to it – there would be no pre-wedding nerves for me. I didn't even read any significance into the fact that none of Steve's family were to attend. My family would certainly make up the numbers, as not only were Mum and Dad and all my cousins going to witness my big day, even my birth-parents were going to be there.

In the registrar's office, I was so happy as I stood next to Steve to take my vows, resplendent in my chic wedding outfit of short white minidress, matching big floppy hat and wedge-platformed shoes. The whole occasion passed by in a blur of excitement. But what Steve failed to realise, and so did I at the time, was that I was viewing the whole notion of marriage through the eyes of a child. I was nothing more than a little girl dressing up as a blushing bride and paying lip service to the solemnity of the commitment I was making. Afterwards, my relatives apparently commented to each other that it had been as if I was play-acting. They all thought I was far too young and immature to make this kind of decision, but I was also a single mother with a little girl to bring up, and they didn't know what other options were available to me – what else was I going to do?

In retrospect, I can see that I had no idea of what true love was. For me, it was more an opportunity to celebrate achieving the legitimacy I craved of becoming a good wife and mother, the perfect housekeeper in the perfect family unit, and I clutched at it with all the optimism of a child. For whilst I may have been in my late teens and my body had grown into that of a young woman, emotionally I had not progressed past the age of about eight or nine, when I first suffered abuse at the hands of my birth-father. I would later come to learn that this is quite common in child victims, as our bodies have suffered a physical assault that mentally we are not programmed to deal with, and emotional growth gets frozen at that point in time.

After the wedding, Steve was initially puzzled about why I didn't want any further contact with my birth-parents. He knew that our relationship had been difficult, but I was not capable of relating all the things Ronald had done to me. I still blamed myself and felt ashamed, so to relive them in such a way would have only made the hurt as raw as the day it had happened. I therefore told him vaguely that Ronald had hurt me as a child and I wanted no more to do with him. Steve was very understanding. He didn't push me for details but simply put his arms around me and said he would take care of me, promising no one would ever hurt me again. These were the words I had been longing to hear, and I believed him with all my heart. He then asked if he could adopt Heidi, and to me this showed just how much he cared for us. When the arrangements were formalised, it meant not only that we were a family all sharing the same name but also that Heidi and I both belonged somewhere at last.

Shortly afterwards, to celebrate passing my driving test and to give me a bit of independence, Steve bought me a wonderful little car, a dark-grey Morris Minor that was odd and quirky, just like me, so we fitted together well. After painting large yellow daisies on the bonnet and doors, it's not surprising I nicknamed her Daisy. But it wasn't the obvious quirks which won my affection, it was all the hidden idiosyncrasies, such as the lack of a left indicator, which meant I had to keep the window wound down at all times so I could make hand signals. There was a button on the floor that you used to dip the headlights, and on many occasions I would end up standing on my feet as I juggled with the clutch, accelerator, brakes and main beam. I could even see the road through the floorboards as I drove along, and I soon learnt not to turn corners too sharply, as the passenger door would suddenly fly open. But, as far as I was concerned, when I was behind the wheel of my first car, I felt like I was driving a Rolls-Royce, and I missed Daisy dearly when she, not surprisingly, failed her MOT just three months after I got her. What I only realised with hindsight was that, purely by coincidence, Daisy's demise coincided with the start of the rapid decline of my marriage. Steve went out and bought me a little Ford Anglia as a replacement, but this was not the only change in store.

No one can choose their in-laws, as I was soon to discover on a trip to Steve's sister's house in Devon, where I was finally introduced to his family. On the surface, they were perfectly polite towards me, but I could not ignore the odd comment that betrayed their true feelings towards Steve's new wife. Perhaps they didn't approve of our marriage because of my age or because I'd been an unmarried teenage mother, but I felt quite relieved when we finally left for home that day.

Despite the rather tense first meeting with my new extended family, I fell in love with the area and was extremely keen when Steve suggested we move to be nearer to his family. After we had found a suitable property in Torquay, I packed for the move as enthusiastically as he did, but what had seemed an ideal move in theory soon proved to be a big mistake. Far away from familiar surroundings and everyone I knew, I was now totally reliant on Steve, and the dynamics of our relationship shifted as dramatically as they did swiftly.

When we first met, I had been his young employee, so he was obviously in the driving seat, but I had assumed that, as our personal relationship had developed, we had been building mutual respect. Now, he was once more the undisputed master, and this manifested itself in an alarming change in his sexual demands. He wanted to explore aspects of this area of our relationship that I didn't feel comfortable with, but I complied initially because he was my husband and I felt I had to do as he wished. Wasn't that what all wives did? I didn't know, as I had no reference point from which to judge what was or was not a 'normal' relationship. I had no friends with whom I could discuss what was going on and felt completely at his mercy. On the occasions when I did resist, Steve became extremely angry and threatened that if I did not submit to his wishes he could always send me back to Ronald and Emily. The prospect of being sent back to my birth-parents filled me with utter dread, but I also realised I'd swapped one bully, in the shape of Ronald, for another. There were many private moments when I would break down and cry. My dream of the perfect family life seemed to dissolve around me as the sinking feeling of being trapped swamped me once more.

I stared out of the window at the lush Devon countryside passing me by as we drove through Dartmouth on our way to a dinner party with Steve's friends. The conversation between us had been rather stilted during the long journey, and this didn't help my nerves much, as I already felt apprehensive at meeting a group of his closest friends. I was eager to impress them but somehow suspected I would fail. Unfortunately, my fears proved well founded, as it became immediately obvious on meeting them that his friends would not accept me, this oddity, into their close circle. I was merely Steve's young wife, with whom they had nothing in common, and I would be tolerated as such. No attempt was made to bridge the gulf between us, which only served to make me feel even more awkward and embarrassed. For the first time in my life, I drank heavily throughout the evening in a bid to numb my increasing anxiety, to the point at which it finally became necessary for me to go in search of a bedroom in which to lie down. I stumbled into a spare room where the guests' coats had been placed on the bed and, snuggling down into them, I felt the room momentarily spin before I finally passed out.

I never heard him enter the room nor was I aware of his presence until a heavy, suffocating weight on top of me shook me from my stupor and the stench of his drunken breath swamped my face. As my vision began to clear in the now brightly lit room, I vaguely recognised the man as one of the people I'd met earlier in the evening. Through the fog of my mind, I was also sure I could hear laughter. Then, as panic seized me, I realised not only that I was now naked but that this stranger was both on top of and inside me. As I turned my head, I could see Steve and his friends all watching and laughing, cheering on the exertions of the man who was raping me. I pushed him off and ran screaming to the corner of the room, snatching a coat off the bed to cover myself up as I went. But as I sat sobbing, the laughter just intensified before another man came to try to pull me to my feet, insisting it was now his turn. It was only then that I heard my husband's voice from the doorway telling them to leave me alone as I'd had enough, so how many there had been before I regained consciousness I have no idea. They all simply turned and walked away, still laughing as they went, leaving me in my shame. I overheard one of Steve's women friends say, 'See, you should have married me, not that young whore.'

I was already awake when dawn's early light peeped through the curtains of the guest room where we lay. I'd barely slept, but it wasn't anger at Steve's cruelty that had robbed me of sleep, it was fear. Every day of my young life I'd been told what a wicked, evil whore I was, and now I was afraid my husband would no longer want such a filthy little tramp for a wife. I stayed in the bedroom when Steve went down for breakfast, and there I remained, deep in my own thoughts, until it was time to leave, which I managed without looking a single person in the face. Nothing was mentioned about the events of the previous night during the long drive home and nor would the subject be raised again. This was much to my relief, as I spent weeks expecting to be thrown out of our home at a moment's notice because of my behaviour. Instead, Steve's brutal sexual demands of me increased to the point where I loathed myself and how filthy I felt.

I was, however, grateful that he still wanted me, and I spent long hours alone in tears as I struggled to come to terms with the confusion that raged within me.

A couple of weeks later, with a sense of deliberate purpose and serenity, I locked all the doors and drew the curtains at the front of the house. The children were all either in school or nursery, and I would not be disturbed for hours, giving me plenty of time to execute the plan I had in mind. The paracetamol tablets clattered like a drum roll across the table's hard surface as I spilled them from their container before breaking the seal on a bottle of vodka. I sat there toying with the tablets, knowing I couldn't go on like this any longer. I thought briefly of my little girl and how she would be better off without me before popping the first bitter pill into my mouth and swallowing it down with a mouthful of the cool clear alcohol, shuddering at the bitter taste. One by one, I made inroads into the pile of pills until I found myself gradually drifting down into a comfortingly dark and velvety space; there was no sense of panic as I slipped into unconsciousness.

The next thing I was aware of was two people trying to walk me around the room, but my legs were like rubber and just wouldn't function. Gradually, I came to and recognised one of those trying to help me as a neighbour I would later find out had become suspicious when I didn't leave to collect the children at the same time I did each day. Instinctively knowing something was amiss, she went around the back of the house and climbed the fence, from where she could see me in the living room hanging over the side of the sofa, and with that she'd raised the alarm. Another neighbour had helped her break in, and it was these two lifesavers who now propped me up. An ambulance was already on its way, and within minutes I was rushed, sirens blaring, to hospital to have my stomach pumped.

After the procedure, my insides felt as if they were on fire, but the greatest pain was the disappointment of knowing I couldn't even kill myself properly. Steve came to see me that evening, but once we were alone, his manner immediately became brusque. Leaning over me where I lay, he hissed at me that if I ever mentioned to anyone what had happened that night at his friends' house he would make sure I was granted my death wish, and the menacing timbre of his voice more than backed up the seriousness of his threat. His words, however, didn't have the desired impact, for what he failed to understand was that I could not remember a period in my life after being snatched by my birth-parents when I hadn't wished I was dead. It may have been at times no more than a deep dark notion lurking around my subconscious, but my mind was constantly tormented and all I wanted was to be rid of the pain and shame inside.

Mum and Dad had by now retired from the shop and were at my bedside as fast as they could get there. They urged me to see a psychiatrist but, as per Steve's instructions, I flatly refused and discharged myself from hospital as soon as I could. My suicide attempt was not mentioned once after my return home, and life returned to what it had been before, as if I'd merely suffered a nasty cold or some similar malady that could easily be shaken off. I pushed this latest shameful episode deep down inside of me, to join all the others I mistakenly thought could be buried so easily.

FOURTEEN

Second Time Around

Turning the ignition key, I was not too surprised when, yet again, the engine of my little blue Ford Anglia let out a flat churning sound. As the car was pretty much on its last legs, it had become a battle of wills to get it started each time, but I had an ace up my sleeve in the shape of a long piece of wood and my trusty hammer, both of which I took with me on all my travels. With the piece of wood positioned at a certain point on the starter motor, a hefty whack or two with the hammer would soon have the engine running. It might not sound very technical, but it usually did the trick, which was just as well as my car had become a lifeline.

Steve's work had increasingly been taking him away from home. He was now abroad for a couple of months and, while the mortgage and bills were taken care of, money for day-to-day living was fast running out, so I had no choice but to find a way of earning some extra cash. Here I was, aged just 18, little more than a child myself, struggling to run a house on my own and look after three young children. When things got too much to bear, I would pack up the children into the car and drive to my mum's, but this got more and more difficult to do as the money ran out and I struggled to afford the petrol. I was desperately lonely, and this was far from the fairy-tale family life that I had originally thought Steve was offering. We hardly even spoke when he was away, due to the exorbitant cost of overseas phone calls and, looking back, it would seem that for Steve I was nothing more than a live-in nanny with extras thrown in.

After accepting the help of a friendly neighbour who offered to babysit for the children, I managed to find an assortment of part-time jobs in an attempt to make ends meet. One of them involved canvassing for a local photographer, which, having knocked on doors for Ronald from a very young age, I was ideally suited to. It was not without its complications, however, as one of my target areas was the army camp a couple of miles away. During one of my trips there, one of the soldiers who answered my knock at his front door asked me for some form of identification. This came as a surprise, as I'd been there a few times before and had no idea I needed a special pass to be on the grounds. I replied that I hadn't any on me and made my way to the next house along to see if they were in need of the services of a professional photographer. Suddenly, an army Land Rover pulled up sharply at the gate and out jumped two rather agitated soldiers demanding to know who I was and what I was doing there. As I was unable to present a special pass, I was swiftly escorted to the guardhouse, where I was locked in a cell. Even though I tried to explain the simple mistake to the interviewing officer, and gave him my boss's contact details, it was many hours before I was finally released and given official identification allowing me on to the camp, which I made sure I never left home without again.

The other part-time position I had at this point was in the cocktail bar of a local hotel. I really enjoyed it as I had to dress up, and it seemed so glamorous to be making cocktails and chatting to the customers in the elegant surroundings of the hotel. One customer in particular was always very charming and sweet towards me, complimenting me not only on my service but also on my looks. I was at such a low ebb as a result of what was happening in my private life, I found myself opening up to this tall handsome stranger called Sean, telling him just how lonely and sad I'd become.

Sean was Irish by birth, and I found his lilting accent very attractive. He worked for a London company which often sent him to Devon on business. During each trip, he would come into the bar after work. I found myself counting the days between each visit as we chatted so freely and openly in each other's company. One evening, after I'd finished my shift, he kindly offered to walk me home, and I did not resist when he took me in his arms and kissed me tenderly. As far as I was concerned, Steve had abandoned me, and I was no longer sure whether he had ever really cared for me. With Sean on the other hand, as our relationship developed I felt that this time it really was true love. He accepted Heidi without question and said how much he wanted to look after us both. When he finally suggested I should leave my husband and start a new life with him, I didn't need much persuasion, but I wanted to tell Steve in person and I couldn't abandon his two little girls so callously.

As the key turned in the front door, I wrung my clammy hands in nervous anticipation. Telling Steve I was leaving him had all seemed so simple and straightforward in my mind, but now that the moment of truth was approaching, I was terrified about how he would react. I leapt from the sofa as he entered the living room carrying his many bags from the trip. My own small suitcase was by my side, and Heidi, who was now three years old, was nearby holding her doll's carrycot. Steve seemed to guess what I was about to say before I uttered a word, but he expressed no anger or upset, merely a cool disdain for his silly little wife who was about to leave him. It seemed to me that, as far as he was concerned, he was losing a possession rather than a wife, and his reaction suggested I would not be missed. With just the clothes I stood up in, my small case of belongings in one hand and holding Heidi's little hand in the other, I walked to Sean's car parked down the road and left with him for London that day without looking back.

We arrived at a hotel in Knightsbridge tired and hungry, but already I felt a certain sense of relief and contentment at having escaped the binds of my unhappy marriage. The hotel was only ever meant as a temporary stopgap, and for the next couple of weeks I delighted in spending my days taking Heidi to all the famous landmarks and other places of interest, soaking up the sights and sounds of the capital city. Within the month, Sean's company had transferred him to Norfolk, where we spent the first eight weeks in another hotel, and once more I spent my days taking Heidi for leisurely strolls, appreciating the contrast between the city's hustle and bustle and the peace and tranquillity of the countryside. We might have been living out of a suitcase, but we did so with the happiness peculiar to the first flush of romance, and Sean was adamant that he wanted us to be married as soon as my divorce came through so we could set up home together and have a child of our own.

He promised that he was going to look after Heidi and me; he would love me for ever and everything was going to be OK. These were the same promises that Steve had made and which I had been so desperate to believe from him only two years earlier. But I was still only 18 years old and couldn't see that I was falling into a pattern in which I rushed headlong into relationships, hoping that this time the man was going to save me; that this time he would believe I was worth saving. All I could see was that we seemed to have the same hopes and dreams, and I revelled in Sean's enthusiasm for our future happiness. Once again, I was placing my life and happiness in someone else's hands, but I believed that this time it would be different, as Sean seemed so different from any of the men I had previously met. There was an empty void within me that I ached to fill with love and approval, and I was desperate for someone to believe that I was worthy of affection and not the vile, evil bitch that Ronald had always told me I was.

Although I hadn't been in touch with him since I'd left, Steve tracked me down and turned up unannounced at the hotel one day whilst Sean was at work. In his steely detached manner, he gave me my instructions on how the divorce would proceed, namely that I was not to ask for any money from him and in return he would have no further role in Heidi's life. As far as I was concerned, I no longer wanted him anywhere near us, and if the price to pay for that freedom was to relinquish any financial claim on Steve, then so be it. I felt a nagging sense of shame at being divorced so young, but I readily agreed to his demands, and I would neither see nor hear from him ever again.

Sean and I invested what little money we had in a new small car, a Hillman Imp and, following a lovely holiday down in Devon, we spent much of our spare time searching for somewhere more permanent to live. Eventually we found a little three-bedroom house in Winterton-on-Sea, and I was thrilled when we picked up the keys to the property. It might only have been furnished with the basics but, as far as I was concerned, it felt like a palace. What appealed to me most about the place was the small but perfectly kept garden, which was a great suntrap, and Heidi enjoyed many hours playing there on the red and blue bicycle Sean bought for her.

She and I were so close during those early years of her life. She was such a gorgeous, well-behaved little girl and was always by my side whether we were out and about or back at home. I remember that while I was doing the ironing, she would stand next to me with her little plastic iron and ironing board, pretending to press the tea towels while chattering away and asking a constant stream of questions. At first Sean seemed to adore her, and we were all so excited when I found out that I had fallen pregnant, Heidi looking forward to having a little brother or sister.

Money remained tight, but it couldn't dampen our enthusiasm as Sean and I planned for the arrival of our baby. Most of the items we bought were second-hand, and I would then spend hours scrubbing and cleaning everything, from the pram to the cot, until my arms ached. I took a great deal of pride in the fact I'd restored these things so they were nearly as good as new. It felt that, unlike during my pregnancy with Heidi, I was now doing all the things a proper mother-to-be might do, and I relished every second of it.

What I could share with Heidi was her first day at school, and I marvelled at how she looked so small yet at the same time so grown up in her uniform. Heidi took to school like a duck to water, and on her return home that first day, my heart leapt to see her so excited and keen to tell me all the wonderful new experiences she'd had.

A few months later, in the early hours of 1 May 1976, my beautiful baby boy made his entrance into the world and, with little Alex there to make everything complete, I felt truly blessed to be with Sean and my children. The day of his christening dawned fine and sunny, and I was delighted that members of Sean's family had been able to make the trip over from Ireland to join with my relatives in celebrating my little boy's special day. I knew that Sean came from a very poor background in Ireland and I appreciated the effort and expense that his parents had gone to in order to meet their new grandson.

Our wedding a few months later was also a family affair, and I felt so proud to have Heidi as my bridesmaid, marvelling at how beautiful she looked in her lilac dress.

I was one bride who truly didn't mind being upstaged on her big day! Soon after the wedding, however, the first cracks began to show in another of my relationships when I started to notice that Sean had acquired an ever-growing taste for alcohol.

I had always known that Sean was fond of a drink – we had, after all, first met in the bar where I'd worked – but his consumption now not only began to exceed what our meagre budget would allow, his temperament also changed and he was seldom the happy-go-lucky drinker he had been in the early days of our courtship. He worked very long hours, and I was loath to criticise his drinking when it seemed to relax him, but increasingly it led to him becoming surly and short-tempered, although at first he was always quick to apologise when his mood soured.

Sean's drinking problem was put to the back of my mind when baby Alex developed a health problem with his penis, and to my shame I was much to blame for the condition that developed. There was nothing I loved more than the comforting smell of baby talcum powder, so whenever I cleaned him, I would sprinkle it liberally and breathe in heavily as the aroma wafted around me. However, I must have used too much as it caused an irritation on the sensitive skin around Alex's penis. When I asked the health visitor about the problem, she suggested that the next time Alex was playing in the bath I should pull the foreskin back and clean around it, as this would solve the problem in no time. It seemed a simple enough solution, and as I ran his bath that evening, I didn't give the prospect of cleaning him intimately a second thought. The moment I came to actually do it, however, a sudden sickening panic arose in me. I started shaking as I felt my face flush and beads of sweat bud on my forehead. I was absolutely terrified at the prospect and, no matter how hard I tried, I found I was simply unable to touch my son in this way. In the end, I gave in, and repeated attempts over the next few days similarly ended in failure. When I went back to the clinic, I admitted that I might not have cleaned Alex properly, but I could not bring myself to tell the health visitor I was not capable of cleaning him there at all. She ticked me off and told me I really must try harder and, with her admonishment ringing in my ears, I returned home close to tears.

For the next few evenings, I felt what was becoming a familiar terror rise in me as I tried to bathe my son. For poor Alex, this resulted in the infected area becoming extremely sore, causing him great upset. I had no option other than to return to the clinic, and when asked if I had been cleaning the infected area, I finally broke down in tears but was unable to explain what the problem was.

What I'd been unable to verbalise was that cleaning Alex in this way disgusted me. It reminded of the horrific bath-times I had endured at Ronald's hands, and it was as if I would be abusing my son in the same way that my birth-father had abused me. The health visitor had no choice but to deal with Alex's medical condition herself and, thankfully, the rash cleared up in a matter of days. She also suggested I should visit my own doctor to see if he could help, as she recognised that there was something going on in my mind that she was not qualified to deal with.

During a lengthy consultation in which I wrung my hands incessantly and many tears were shed, I finally managed to tell my doctor that my birth-father had interfered with me as a child and that was why I could not touch my own son. It felt wrong, and no matter how hard I tried to overcome this seemingly irrational thought, I knew I would not be able to change the way I felt. It was by no means a full and frank confession of all that had happened to me as a child, but it was significant in that it was the first time I had told anyone so much, and I felt truly spent when I'd finished.

Although I was unaware of it at the time, my suicide attempt during my marriage to Steve must have been included on my medical notes and, as I was obviously still in some distress, my doctor suggested a radical form of therapy that perhaps might help my mental outlook. It was the first time anyone had recognised there was a link between the events of my childhood and the state of my mental health, and initially I was relieved that there might be something that could be done to help me.

The phrase 'electric shock treatment' meant little to me but, though my doctor offered no further explanation, I did not object to his suggestion and was referred for a session at the local hospital. On the morning of the first appointment, my neighbour kindly offered to look after the children while Sean was at work, and I went to the hospital alone. Once there and in the treatment room, I was given no explanation of what to expect, no reassuring words to ease the ever-growing anxiety I was beginning to experience. Instead, I was strapped down to a bed by my arms and legs, something damp was placed on my forehead and a strap was put in my mouth in case I needed to bite down on something. This terrified me but, as at so many times in my life when I was told something must happen, I complied unquestioningly. It was as if I had slipped into some freeze-mode, like a rabbit caught in headlights, unable to react or object to what was being done to me.

After the treatment had begun, I lost all further memory of that day. I can't even remember how I returned home, and the six or so follow-up sessions were similarly a blur. To this day, I cannot say if I received any benefits from the electric shock treatment, and in my darker hours I cannot help but wonder if it partially blocked out the horror of other things that might have happened to me, leaving me unable to deal with them and put them to rest.

While going through this traumatic experience, I also had more problems to deal with on the home front, as Sean had begun to spend money we simply didn't have like it was going out of fashion. Not only were the children regularly treated to new clothes and toys, new furniture for the house also started to arrive at frequent intervals. To make matters worse, Sean had also developed a gambling habit. Each day, the post would include yet another bill, and their arrival served to perpetuate a vicious circle whereby Sean would go out and get drunk and buy even more expensive items we neither needed nor could afford.

With Heidi being at school, at least she could have her main meal of the day there during the week and similarly Sean could eat at work. Alex, meanwhile, lived off the powdered or puréed meals I made myself with whatever ingredients were to hand, whilst my diet consisted mainly of porridge. This helped to eke out the finances a little bit further, but it did not address the root problem, a problem Sean numbed himself to with increasingly frequent bouts of heavy drinking. In the end, I had no choice but to go out and find work, and that autumn I got an evening job behind the bar of the local village pub. It seemed the most obvious choice, as Sean could take on the child-care duties in the evenings.

My husband, however, was not best pleased with the decision I'd made. He believed it diminished his status as head of the household and implied that he was not in a position to provide for his wife and family. He managed to soothe his injured male pride with yet more drink, and often I would return home late at night after completing my shift only to find Sean passed out on the sofa, oblivious to the cries of the children upstairs and the pool of vomit in which he lay. On other occasions, he would still be awake, but with his aggression fuelled by alcohol, it was only ever a matter of moments before he would start a row. His argument was that he only drank heavily because I left him at home on his own with the children so often, and on the one occasion I dared to state that if he didn't spend so much on his bottles of whisky then I wouldn't have to go out to work in the evenings, a terrible row erupted.

I could see no benefit in continuing the argument, so I went upstairs to change Alex. I could hear Sean's drunken, misplaced footsteps behind me as he tried to climb the stairs in pursuit, and when I came out of Alex's room onto the landing holding the baby, Sean lunged at us in an attempt to grab his son. In doing so, he knocked me sideways down the stairs with Alex still in my arms. As I spun, I somehow managed to wrap my arm around the rope handrail. It broke my fall and, miraculously, neither Alex nor I was hurt, but we were both frightened. Alex's screams seemed to register with Sean, as he was absolutely mortified by what he had done and rushed to our aid.

For the next few days, all was quiet. Sean cut back on his drinking, and we even took the children on a picnic and laughed a lot in the sunshine as we played with them. Sean promised me things would be different from now on and, in that happy moment, all I wanted to do was believe him. However, it proved to be merely a lull in the storm.

My drunken husband was soon no longer content with confining our rows to within the walls of the family home; he would often arrive at the pub and cause a drunken scene there, too, and it was only a matter of time before the landlord asked me to leave. I did manage to get bar work at another pub in the village but, however much we might have needed the extra income, I was becoming increasingly uneasy at leaving Sean in charge of the children. Each night before I went to work, he promised me he wouldn't drink to excess; and each night on my return, I found that he had. I'd also finally discovered how he'd been funding his alcohol addiction, as the bills I'd assumed he'd paid were returning as final notices either threatening to cut us off or with a visit from the bailiffs. Eventually I confided in the only close friend I had made in the area – Wendy – and, in a bid to outfox the bailiffs, she kindly offered to let me store anything of value in her house, an offer that I gratefully accepted.

Whether by accident or by design, Sean made it increasingly difficult for me to show up for work as he was spending more and more time away from home, allegedly on business. On one occasion, he'd failed to return by the time he'd promised, making it impossible for me to go to work, and in the pit of my stomach, I knew something was very wrong. Many panic-stricken hours passed before I finally heard his key in the front-door lock. When he walked in, he stood there holding his stomach and had various cuts and grazes criss-crossing his face. Rather shamefaced, he explained that he had rolled his car on a tight bend on the outskirts of the village, crashing first into a ditch and then into a tree, leaving the car a total write-off. Police at the scene had breathalysed him and, of course, he was well over the limit.

On another occasion, when I had been able to make it to the pub, I returned to find the front door wide open and Heidi locked in her room, so frightened that she had wet herself. Alex's nappy was also soaked through and both of them were crying their little hearts out. Sean went missing for days after this, which meant I couldn't work. As ever, he returned full of apologies, which in his sober state I believe were quite sincere, but it was clear his drinking problem was not going to resolve itself. I secretly contacted Al-Anon, a support group for the relatives and friends of alcoholics, who gave me as much support as they could, but told me that, ultimately, Sean had to realise for himself that he had a problem. In my heart of hearts, I knew that would never happen and, as his drunken outbursts spiralled out of control, I just didn't know how much more I could take.

Looking back, I also now realise that his behaviour had a serious effect on Heidi, who was by now old enough to sense that there was something wrong. The relationship between her and Sean had already suffered after Alex's birth, as he doted on his son and took little further interest in Heidi. She was initially very interested in her brother, but Sean kept telling her to leave the baby alone, and on one occasion he unfairly accused her of intentionally trying to hurt Alex, which upset her deeply.

My mum had given me a recipe for home-made ginger beer, which I made and stored in Coke bottles in the shed at the bottom of the garden. One day, when I was moving them inside to the fridge, Heidi wanted to help, but she dropped one and it exploded on the path. Shards of glass went everywhere, and Alex was cut on his mouth and around his forehead. When Sean came home, he was incensed and ranted and raved at her about what she had done.

Heidi was also sometimes fussy about her food, as all children can be, and this infuriated Sean, perhaps because of the poverty of his own childhood. If she didn't eat what was on her plate, she wasn't allowed to leave the table, and he would make her stay there for hours, ignoring my pleas for him to allow her to get up.

As the situation at home deteriorated, so did Heidi's behaviour, though I am sad to say that at the time I didn't realise that there was a link. She withdrew into herself and became very sullen but, consumed as I was by all the other problems that we faced, I thought that she was simply being difficult and attention-seeking because of her new brother. I can only wish now that I had been able to see what was really going on in my little girl's mind.

FIFTEEN

A Father Figure

I couldn't help but notice him, with his well-built frame and shock of red hair. He might have been much older than me, as he was in his late 40s, but he moved with such self-assured confidence and muscular grace that he caught the eye of everyone in the pub – and he was well aware of the fact, too. Each Saturday night, Dave sang in the pub where I now worked. He always made a point of talking to me behind the bar before the pub became too busy, which it always did during Dave's performances, and my heart skipped a beat to have the attention of this smooth, good-looking man. I was even more flattered when he began offering to drive me home at the end of the night. I might have been married to Sean for only the past six months or so but, with everything that had happened, I was already looking for a way out of the relationship, and I couldn't resist being the envy of every woman in the pub as I stepped into Dave's car for the ride home.

These lifts happened on a few occasions, and we

would chat easily before bidding each other goodnight. That was until one evening when he reached across and kissed me passionately, and I couldn't help but kiss him back. Embarrassed by what I'd done, I muttered my excuses and left, entering the house with my heart all a-flutter only to be greeted by the sight of Sean yet again snoring on the sofa.

The following Saturday, the bar was absolutely packed with customers, and Dave was entertaining them with his usual repertoire of favourites. I could barely hear the customer who leaned over the bar to tell me my husband was at the door wanting to speak to me and could I pop outside for a moment. Something had to be amiss, as Sean was supposed to have been at home looking after the children. As I raced for the door, my first thought was that something must have happened to one of them.

When I opened the door of the public bar, however, I knew immediately what the problem was, as I saw Sean slumped up against the wall between the public toilets and the main door. He was a pitiful sight as he slurred his order for me to buy him a bottle of drink and bring it out to him. As I refused, I could smell the alcoholic fumes emanating from him in waves, and I asked him who was looking after Heidi and Alex. In an instant, he seemed to regain the strength in his limbs, his brow knotted into a frown and he roared, 'Fuck the children', before shoving me forcefully towards the bar door and ordering me to get him his bottle of whisky. I shrugged off his grip and told him that I couldn't serve him, only for him to start shouting menacingly before he began slapping me about the head and then punched me full in the stomach, much in the same way Ronald used to do. Breathless from the blow, I watched him lurch out of the main door as a crowd of onlookers, who had seen Sean strike me but been too slow to intervene, suddenly surrounded me.

The landlord kindly let me go home early, and I was not altogether surprised to find the front door wide open when I arrived, though at least the children were asleep in their beds. After checking on them, I rushed downstairs and put the chain on the door so that Sean could not get back in, then I went back upstairs, scooped my two sleeping children out of their beds and put them in mine, laying one on either side of me so I could wrap an arm around each as I kept alert for my husband's return.

My attempts to keep Sean out proved unnecessary, as he did not return for days, by which time he had sobered up and was once more full of apologies, but the assault in the pub had moved the situation on to a level I could not tolerate. It was too late for me to forgive him, and I knew I had to leave.

Having lived out of a suitcase for so long when Sean and I first ran away together, the prospect of returning to such a life did not appeal to me much, but it held no fears either. I'd already made enquiries around the village about accommodation and had found a vacant bedsit in a very old house at the back of a baker's shop just off the main street. The property consisted of a front sitting room upstairs (which would have to double up as my bedroom), a further room for the children to share and a small bathroom. There was an unused room downstairs as well as a tiny kitchen in need of a good clean, but the main problem was that the building had no heating and I could actually see daylight through the walls in places. Nevertheless, it would serve its purpose, and when Sean next left on a business trip, I hastily bundled whatever possessions I had into the back of a van that I had borrowed for a couple of hours and made good my escape with the children.

I was under no illusions. I knew Sean would easily be able to track us down, but the harsh rapping at the front door about a week later still caused my heart to pound. Against my better judgement, I opened the door to him before he disturbed the whole street with his shouting. From the doorstep, Sean begged me to come back with the children, promising yet again how everything would be better now and that he would never act in a violent way towards me again. His hollow words made no impact on me this time, however, and sensing defeat Sean's male pride came surging to the fore. It was one thing for his wife to go out to work but for his wife to leave him was intolerably shameful. Sean's brow furrowed as he spat out his threat to snatch Alex from me and take him to Ireland if I didn't return with the children at once. At that, I slammed the door in his face and went to offer and find comfort in the company of my two scared children.

It was by no means the end of the matter, however, as Sean took to following me menacingly down the street at every opportunity, and he even tried to break into my flat, which was absolutely terrifying. In the end, I had no option other than to approach a solicitor and file for an injunction order to keep my estranged husband from stalking me in this manner. Thankfully, the threat of legal action seemed to do the trick.

One much more welcome and frequent visitor during these traumatic times was Dave, to whom I increasingly clung for support. As our relationship developed, I suppose I viewed him as a father figure, the father I had never had. He seemed so strong and confident, and I felt cared for and protected in his presence. This time, he really did seem to be offering me the happiness I so desperately craved but had begun to think would always remain tantalisingly out of reach, and whenever I saw his handsome figure, my heart leapt with joy.

Dave was not free to visit me as often as I would have liked in those early days as he still lived with his wife, but he assured me the marriage was over and he only stayed for his children's sake, two boys in their late teens. Although I wished his wife no harm, I could barely contain my happiness when he finally left her and moved into a flat not too far away from mine.

However, I could no longer cope with the icy draughts that ventilated my own cramped bedsit. It wasn't a healthy environment for the children and Alex developed whooping cough, which took a long time to shift. The three of us would often spend our evenings and weekends curled up in the sofa bed I slept on, in an attempt to keep warm, and I made regular appeals to the council to help us find another home. Fortunately they found us a house not too far away, so that Heidi didn't have to change schools, lessening the impact of another upheaval for her.

My little council house was a home made in heaven as far as I was concerned. With its large rear garden set out to vegetables and soft fruit, complete with a small greenhouse, it reminded me so much of my brief but happy childhood years at Shepherds Lane. I delighted in growing my own seedlings and tomatoes, the heady aroma of which brought so many memories flooding back, and after acquiring a second-hand freezer, I took to preserving whole batches of home-grown produce. The long galley kitchen resembled something out of a country farmhouse as I began making my own bread and thick fruity jams, whilst my two children never went short of homemade ice lollies or the warm doughy results of my daily baking.

Money was rather tight, and I knew whatever I had I would have to make last, although matters were helped somewhat after the house that Sean and I had shared was repossessed and sold. Once all the creditors had been paid, there was still a little sum for me, which helped me buy a few items for my new home. I also bought some new suits for Dave for his act, as I wanted him to share in my modest windfall. Whatever the state of my finances, spiritually I had never felt so well off. I loved the fact that the children were now able to help me in the garden, tending to their own special flowerbed just as I had done as a youngster. While Alex was too young to fully understand all I tried to teach them, Heidi, now aged seven, seemed to absorb it all like a sponge, and for a while her behaviour seemed to improve. Now that I wasn't consumed with Sean and his drinking, I was able to give her more of the attention that she craved. She didn't seem too impressed by the arrival of a new man in our lives, though, and she and Dave never really got along.

Soon after I'd settled into my new home, Dave

suggested we all went away on holiday together to stay for a week in a caravan near Great Yarmouth. I don't know who was more excited, me or the children. Even Heidi got caught up in the happy mood, and laughter filled the house as we packed our sunglasses, hats, buckets and spades in preparation for what would be a wonderful holiday, taking in the bracing sea air on beachfront walks to whet our appetites for chips smothered in salt and vinegar.

When Dave asked me on our return if he could move in with me, I didn't hesitate for a second. I was only twenty-two years old and already had two failed marriages behind me, but once again I managed to convince myself that this was my chance of happiness; I had to grab on to it and never let it go. This time I was determined not to mess up the relationship, for at the back of my mind I couldn't help but feel that Steve would have treated me better and Sean could have given up drinking if only I had been a better wife. If I'd only tried harder, if I'd only been good enough – these feelings of inadequacy and guilt would dog me throughout my life. Whenever anything went wrong, I blamed myself, and it is only now I realise that the roots of these feelings were firmly planted in the abuse my birth-father subjected me to.

This time, I certainly wasn't going to make the same mistakes with Dave, and as my new-look family settled down to life together, I made sure things couldn't have been sweeter. We loved living by the sea, and I spent many happy hours down on the beach with the children as they rode their bikes up and down the path along the sea wall, giggling as the spray from a breaking wave sprinkled them. Whole days were spent crabbing or collecting shells and stones that caught the eye. Even when the weather was bad, we'd still be found by the seafront, making hot reviving cups of tea on a little stove whilst the children wore themselves out exploring. Often of an evening, Heidi and I would climb onto our bikes, with Alex sitting in a special seat on the back on mine, and cycle down the quiet country back lanes, and if the day hadn't already been spent picking fruit or vegetables at a local farm – strawberries forever remaining the favourite – we would spend ages picking blackberries from the hedgerows. One in the mouth and three into the basket seemed to be the general rule, and Alex and Heidi would return home with their mouths and fingers stained from the juices of their evening feast, marks which would still be visible the following day no matter how hard you scrubbed.

One of the happiest times the children and I spent together was one summer holiday when we decided to visit my aunt Grace, aunt Lily and uncle Tom, who by now lived far away out in the rugged Cornish countryside. I was delighted when Mum was able to join me, Heidi and Alex, along with my cousin Heather and her four children, Sally, Susan, Lily and baby Emma. I drove the Transit van that we had borrowed, with Heather next to me doing the map-reading, while Mum sat in the back on a long bench and occupied the children – no mean feat on such an epic journey. We set off long before the crack of dawn, with the children sleeping on mattresses on the floor under piles of blankets to keep out the night's chill, and we arrived at Stonehenge by the time the sun rose. Wiping the sleep from our eyes, we all marvelled at the shafts of bright sunlight streaming through the stones of this ancient structure.

Despite the ungodly hour, we were by no means the only travellers there to take in the sunrise at such an atmospheric location, and I couldn't help but chuckle at the looks on the other people's faces when I opened up the van's back door and a seemingly endless stream of children flowed out, followed by my mum! With the little 'troops' assembled, we pulled out the old bench and placed it a little way away before erecting several windbreakers around the back door. Then, in no time at all, we were munching on thickly buttered and deep-filled sandwiches, reviving ourselves and warming our hands on mugs of hot steaming tea. It would become a regular sight for anyone who happened to see us on our travels over the next two weeks. Inside the cab, there was a lid between the front seats, under which was the engine. On wet days, this warm lid became the hub of operations: we did everything on it, from buttering the thick slices of bread for our sandwiches to potty-training baby Emma.

None of us had much money to spend, but that fortnight spent with Aunt Grace was a magical time that none of us could have enjoyed more. Sun or rain, we were at the beach or some other place to see the sights, and on one of our daily excursions, we decided to take the children to see the wild seals who'd made a local beauty spot their home. However, it soon became one of those trips when Heather's map-reading skills came under harsh scrutiny, and in no time at all we became lost amongst the maze of narrow country lanes bordered by high hedges. When at last we appeared to be going the right way, we were confronted by a car approaching us from the opposite direction just as the road had become far too narrow to allow two vehicles to pass each other. I had no choice but to pull in to one side to allow the other driver to pass, but as I did so, there was a crunching sound that sent shivers down all of our spines. I had managed to get the van's large wing mirror hopelessly caught up in the roots of a bush on the side of the high-banked lane.

Heather slipped into action, sliding open the van's large side door and struggling with the roots in an attempt to untangle us, but as I started up the engine and tried to pull away, the bank crumbled and an avalanche of red mud cascaded into the van on the passenger side. Soon, Heather was up to her ankles in the stuff, and it seemed we were to be buried alive if the entire bank collapsed. I don't mind admitting I was very frightened and, to make matters worse, the wing mirror was by now even more tangled up. It was obvious any attempt to move off would only compound the problem, so we had no option but to flag down a passing vehicle – which took a while in such an isolated place – and ask the driver to help us. Yet once the crisis had passed, one of us started giggling at our predicament and that set everybody off laughing until our sides ached. We laughed even harder the same day when I missed the turning again, and we never did get to see those seals.

Mum and Dad joined Dave, myself and the children on another holiday, and not only was it wonderful to be with my parents in the large caravan we'd rented again up in Great Yarmouth, but on this particular vacation I was also to realise a childhood dream. I'd loved to dance since those earliest days spent prancing around the vacuum cleaner to the sounds of the radio, but I'd never considered myself adept at the art. However, Dave had taught me the basics of jiving and how to jitterbug, and whilst we were on holiday, he persuaded me we should enter the local dance competition for which we'd spotted a poster.

I had great fun as we twisted and turned our way through the other couples on the dance floor, but I had no expectations of winning. During the course of the evening, however, it became clear that Dave and I had a realistic chance of picking up the first prize, and as the judges called for hush before they announced the winners, I could feel myself shaking like a leaf with fear and expectation. When he read out our names as the winning couple and asked us to take the floor for our solo dance, I couldn't help but soak up the applause and blushed with pure pleasure as we glided across the floor.

Back at home, I once again concentrated on proving myself to be the perfect housewife and homemaker. I believed everything was running smoothly, therefore the whole family must be as happy as I was. However, wrapped up as I was in my perpetual quest to maintain my own personal happiness, I had failed to spot the dark clouds beginning to form on the horizon.

Heidi, now aged nine, was starting to become increasingly difficult. I had written off the change in her behaviour during my marriage to Sean as jealousy over her new brother. In the past, we had spent a lot of time together, with me trying my best to teach her how to bake or sew, or drawing pictures and playing with her favourite toy, the Lego set, and I thought I'd behaved towards her much as my beloved mother had towards my cousins and me. I knew I was a pale shadow of what my mum had been like, but I really did think that I had tried my best. Perhaps I had been deluding myself, however, and my motherly skills were in truth sorely lacking, as Heidi wanted less and less to do with Dave or me. She always seemed to be standing on the outside looking in and would not become involved in any family activity that was taking place.

Heidi had also developed some strange behavioural traits, such as throwing herself through doorways and claiming someone on the other side had pushed her, but rather than its being some childish game, she seemed to be very angry when she said this. She started to self-harm and would pinch herself, leaving welts on her arms. When we were out, she would drag behind or refuse point-blank to walk with us; she would no longer obey either Dave or myself over anything and seemed to take delight in causing problems over the slightest things as well as picking on her younger brother at every opportunity. I thought she was just being naughty for the sake of it, but really she was desperately seeking attention. I'd failed to spot this, as I'd been so absorbed trying to fill my own need for the same. Dave didn't get involved with disciplining her, seeing it as my role to bring up the children while he went out to work to provide for us. They never became close and there was a huge difference between the way he treated Heidi and Alex. Alex was his blue-eyed boy, and he would take him fishing or to play football in the park, while he virtually ignored Heidi, seeing her as a surly and difficult little girl.

With all the information that is available for modern parents, it would probably have been obvious to anyone how unsettled Heidi had been by the series of replacement father figures she'd had due to my failed relationships. There had been little or no stability in her short life, and she craved some time with me on her own, to know that she was important to me. I, however, was obsessed with making this new relationship work and did not make the time for her that she needed. It is hardly surprising that she was resentful of Dave's presence, and it is obvious to me now that her increasingly disturbed behaviour was a cry for help and love.

I turned to Mum for advice and she made suggestions that I put into practice, but to no avail. I became frustrated with Heidi as she pushed me further and further away on all levels. Then I started to become angry with myself and at my life, and this discontent manifested itself in a number of blazing rows with Dave, after which I would feel so full of remorse and self-loathing, as my birth-father Ronald's accusations from my childhood began to return increasingly to haunt me. I'd been a bad daughter and now I was a bad wife and mother, thoroughly rotten beneath the mask of respectable housewife I'd fixed firmly in place for the world at large to see. No matter how I tried, I would never be able to do anything right.

I even thought that perhaps the two miscarriages I suffered in quick succession around this time were a just punishment for my crimes. The doctors told me the second baby had been dead inside me for a week, and whilst the procedure to remove it caused little discomfort, the emotional pain this caused me was overwhelming. When I returned home, I felt as if a part of me had died too, and in time-honoured fashion I immediately started to blame myself. I had no idea how Dave felt at losing these unborn babies, as he never spoke about it, and I was beginning to realise he was not such a pillar of strength when it came to emotional support. He had little sympathy for me as I fell into depression, and his advice was that I should just get over it. Instead, I found myself pushing Dave and the children further away from me – not that Heidi came near me very often anyway. Life merely continued in this limbo-like state, and all I could do was hope that it would somehow return to the happy times that were all too fast becoming distant memories.

SIXTEEN

A Recurring Nightmare

Even during the long drive down to Truro I'd felt in control of the situation, but as I sat parked at the entrance to the drive of this smart little bungalow on the outskirts of town, I felt the familiar fears rising within me, and I needed a moment to compose myself. The children, dressed in their smartest outfits and having been warned to be on their best behaviour, were getting restless and wanted to know why we were just sitting in the car as the persistent and wintry rainfall tapped at the windows. I knew I had to make my decision soon. I just hoped that at the moment of truth my resolve would not weaken.

So much had happened since I'd lost the second baby and all of it had been good. I'd fallen pregnant again, and once I'd reached the 12-week mark with no complications, I finally allowed myself to enjoy my pregnancy without fear of it ending in heartache. I started to look forward to the joy of bringing another baby into the world, and Dave seemed as delighted as I was at the prospect of becoming a parent again. I didn't hesitate for a second when he asked me to marry him, so, at three months gone in the spring of 1981, I walked down the aisle for the third time, with more hope than expectation that everything would work out all right this time around.

All the signs were good when I gave birth to our beautiful daughter Megan in July that year and, like myself, Dave couldn't have been more proud or delighted. He didn't see anything of his two grown-up sons, as they were still angry with him for leaving their mother, so to have a little girl of his own meant a great deal to him. We had become what I had always considered to be the perfect family unit: we had a home, a car and three beautiful children, and we were financially stable.

Buoyed by my improved circumstances, and feeling that I was finally in control of my life, I'd made what I regarded as a positive decision to take the children to see their natural grandparents about a year after Megan had been born. Perhaps Ronald would at last be proud of me, as I had grown up to be a respectable married woman with a family of her own; perhaps at last he would grant me the approval I subconsciously craved. I'd lost contact with Ronald and Emily, but Mum had their new address, and I wrote to them to say we would be coming down.

After taking a deep breath, I plucked up the necessary courage and helped the children get out of the car but, with Megan in my arms, my legs felt less than sturdy as we took the few short steps up to the front door, which Emily answered. I couldn't help but notice the growing number of grey hairs she now had and the lines which appeared on her face as she smiled to greet us, but I appreciated how warm and welcoming she was as she ushered us inside and into the living room. Yet even Emily's warmth did little to thaw the frosty reception Ronald had reserved for me. As Emily busied herself fussing over the children or offering refreshments, my birth-father could do nothing but moan incessantly about what a bad daughter I was for not helping my poor deaf parents. Not once did he even look at the children, his own grandchildren; they may as well not have been there at all.

I certainly had not come to provoke an argument and remained passively mute as Ronald berated me, but I was ready to leave within minutes of meeting him again. I gave Emily some photographs of her grandchildren that I'd put into a small album and made my preparations to leave. As we headed for the door, Emily reached for her purse to give the children a few pennies to share for sweets on the trip home. Ronald immediately leapt to his feet, knocking the coins from his wife's hands as he turned to yell at me that my children were all bastards who had nothing to do with him. I was furious, but it was an impotent rage, and I turned to leave without saying another word, determined to put as much distance as possible between my tormentor and me as quickly as I could.

Silent tears streamed from my eyes for the entire return journey, and I ignored Heidi's questions about the strange angry man who had shouted at me and made such odd noises. I felt that I had shown Ronald the best that I could do, and he had smacked me in the face. I still wasn't good enough.

The disappointment I felt at his rejection was crushing, but cutting Ronald and Emily out of my life was eased considerably by the fact that Dave and I had recently moved and we had much to look forward to. I had been a touch sad to leave behind my little house and garden for our new home with a river view in a quaint little village near the Broads, but I appreciated the adventure the move offered us all. Family bliss seemed all but assured when my mum, dad and brother Robert moved into a house nearby, and for the first time since I was seven years old I had my beloved family around me permanently. Dad had been suffering another bout of ill-health, and as my brother was unhappy in his job, I had suggested that they move close by so that I could help to take care of him. Robert easily found new work, and to have them so close gave me a perpetual warm glow of comfort. On the surface, the future couldn't have looked brighter. But things were about to take a turn for the worse.

Dave threw himself into his singing work, and increased bookings meant he was performing most Thursday, Friday and Saturday evenings. With Mum and Dad more than happy to look after the three children, I was free for the first time in my life to get dressed up and go out for the evening with my husband. I relished every second of this newfound freedom and basked in the glow of Dave's performances. He was ever the showman, and it was extremely exciting to see him in his element, although I have to admit to the odd twinge of jealousy as I watched him flirt with any number of girls and young women and they in turn with him. When I voiced my concerns, Dave was quick to tell me to grow up and not to be so stupid, an accusation of immaturity he was beginning to make on a frequent basis, and with the difference in our ages, I conceded without question.

However, my concerns over my husband's flirtatious behaviour soon proved to be a mere ripple on calm waters, for whilst the house move was supposed to signal a fresh start for us all, Heidi, now 13, had other ideas and her increasingly uncontrollable behaviour caused more rows between Dave and me than anything else. A typical example of her behaviour took place one Sunday lunchtime when I was dishing up the meal and passing it through the serving hatch into the dining room. Heidi was being very helpful, passing the plates around for me, and whilst doing so she asked if she could go out with her friend that afternoon, knowing full well the whole family were meant to be going out together. When told that she couldn't go, she let out the blood-curdling scream that had become all too common in our household and in her temper launched a full plate at the wall, sending pieces of broken china and chunks of food all over the room.

Heidi was prone to such screaming fits whenever she couldn't get her own way, or at any other slight provocation, and while in the throes of her rage she would often scratch both sides of her face with her fingernails until she drew blood. And her wish to inflict pain was by no means confined to acts of self-harm. She was becoming increasingly physical with both of her younger siblings, and the pair of them could often be found in tears because their elder sister had hit them or hurt them in some other way. All children have their disagreements, but Heidi's confrontations were not in the same league as those I remembered with my brother or cousins when I was a child; hers were invariably spiteful and executed with a degree of hatred I had not known my child was capable of, as Alex was to find to his cost walking home from school one day.

I could see he was in some distress when he arrived back home clutching his stomach. He claimed he was suffering from a tummy ache after someone had pushed him on the way home, and it was only later I was to discover from a neighbour that Heidi had been seen viciously punching her little brother in the stomach and taunting him by daring Alex to tell on her. On another occasion, I witnessed Alex politely ask to use the scissors Heidi had by the side of her, and she immediately threw them straight at him, narrowly missing his face.

Alex was not the only target of his elder sister's frustrations, and it was an incident of cruelty involving two-and-a-half-year-old Megan that finally brought matters to a head. I'd been delighted when Heidi had asked me if she could take Megan for a walk, as it was lovely to see her taking an interest in her little sister, but when the pair of them returned an hour or so later Megan was inconsolable. When I checked her arms, I was horrified to see dark blistered skin that looked very much like it had been repeatedly burnt with a cigarette. Despite the shock at seeing my baby girl injured in this way, I was loath to jump to conclusions, and as I tended to Megan's injuries and wiped away her tears, I desperately wanted to believe Heidi's excuse that Megan had wandered off and fallen over into a lawn mower owned by her friend's father. Nevertheless, my nagging doubts would not subside, and I felt compelled to phone this friend's parents just to confirm Heidi's story, only to be told that my daughters had not even been to their home that afternoon.

Something inside me snapped, and I slapped Heidi very hard before sending her to bed. I was at my wits' end: what on earth could have possessed her to bully her own sister in such a sadistic manner? Heidi was certainly not going to give me the answers, as she became even more tight-lipped and withdrawn following her punishment, so I decided that at the first opportunity I would look through her belongings for any clue as to why she was behaving in this way.

The old shoebox she kept under her bed was as good a place as any to start. After lifting its lid, I rummaged through some of Heidi's personal belongings and was shocked to the core at what I found. In each of the photographs she stored in her bedroom, Heidi had scratched out her own face. When I asked her why she had done this, she couldn't give me an answer and became aggressively angry, screaming at me that I had no right to go through her things.

In desperation, I confided in my health visitor, who in turn referred me to a social worker. I was very uncomfortable about the situation, as it started to dredge up unwelcome memories from my past that I had tried so hard to suppress, and I felt a huge sense of shame that I wasn't able to help or control my own daughter. I had tried so hard to build and maintain the façade that we were the perfect family, changing Heidi and Alex's surnames by deed poll in an attempt to hide the embarrassment I felt at my failed marriages and the fact that I had three children by three different fathers. I knew that if the authorities became involved we would have to air a lot of dirty laundry in public, and while I was deeply unhappy about this, I didn't know what else to do.

A counselling session was arranged for both Heidi and myself, but just getting her to attend was a battle of wills. Once there, she refused to cooperate, sitting in a staunch, stony silence. I had no choice but to fill the awkward gaps in conversation, which I did by explaining that if any blame should be apportioned for my daughter's behaviour, then it was all mine. As the conversation progressed down this route, I confessed, in a somewhat stuttering manner, to being not only a bad mother but also a bad person and briefly mentioned my own unhappy childhood. I didn't have the words at that time to describe everything that had happened to me, and wouldn't have wanted to go into detail in front of my daughter anyway, but it was sufficient for the counsellor to suggest I discuss these issues with Dave, so he would have the opportunity to be more supportive. I had previously tried to broach the subject with my husband, but his obvious reluctance to discuss such a subject caused its own frictions, and there was a clear rift growing between us.

After the first joint session, Heidi and I would meet with our own counsellors once a week, but it quickly became clear that these meetings were proving to be of little benefit to Heidi. The social worker obviously spotted some potential help to be offered to me, however, and I would continue with them long after Heidi stopped going. The counsellor suggested I might benefit from writing to Ronald to challenge him about his past crimes and explain the damaging long-term effects they had had on me. This suggestion offered me a way to confront him, which I had never even considered before.

In order to communicate with Ronald as his eyesight got worse, you had to be at a certain angle so that he could see you and you could get his attention. So, if he didn't want to acknowledge what you were saying to him, he would just turn away. This time, however, he would not be able simply to turn his back, and to a certain degree such knowledge was empowering. Many drafts ended up screwed into a ball and plonked in the litter bin until I was finally happy with what I had written. I told him that what he had done to me as a child was wrong and that he must know this. He had hurt me, both when I was younger and then again when I took my children to see him, but he would never get the chance to do it again. I was done and I never wanted to see him again.

As I dropped the envelope into the letterbox, I experienced a mixture of feelings. I was frightened by the thought of finally standing up to him, but there was also a sense of satisfaction about the fact that I was seizing back a little bit of control over my life. I neither expected nor would I receive a reply, but it was none the less gratifying for that.

The situation at home, however, continued to deteriorate, with Heidi's temper getting the better of her on a daily basis and often resulting in Alex and Megan clinging to my legs wide-eyed and terrified. Her mood swings led me to suspect that Heidi was now sniffing glue, as she had been seen hanging around with a group of youths who were known for this. I had no concrete proof she was also involved; all I knew for certain was that drastic measures were called for before our family fell apart at the seams.

In a bid to give us all a little breathing space and try to find out what might be wrong with Heidi, the social worker suggested that she go to an assessment centre for a six-week period. I was horrified by the suggestion that my daughter needed to be taken away from me, but all the experts were saying that this was the best thing to do. They said that Heidi and I needed a break from one another in order to calm down, and that once she was away from her home environment, it would be easier for them to assess what was causing her behaviour. Eventually, they persuaded me that this was the best course of action. Though the decision to send Heidi away was by no means taken lightly, it had become a necessary evil in as much as it allowed life at home to settle down for the other children, who were literally petrified of their elder sister.

I am ashamed to confess that I could not bring myself to visit my daughter at the centre. I was so angry with her, and with my own failings as a mother, that I tried to convince myself that she would be better to have a complete break from me for a short time. This sounds so callous now and, looking back, I think the decision was more to do with my own feelings than with concern over Heidi. The thought of visiting her in a care institution brought back unbearable memories from my childhood, so instead of confronting them and considering how my behaviour had affected my daughter, I pushed everything to the back of my mind and tried to continue with life as normal. All my prayers for an improvement in Heidi's behaviour fell on stony ground, for when the assessment period came to an end she was, perhaps unsurprisingly, more uncontrollable than ever.

As it wasn't possible for her to stay at the centre any longer, social services suggested that Dave and I should consider her being taken into foster care with people who had the necessary experience to deal with problem children. For this to happen, Heidi would have to officially become a ward of court and, remembering my own sense of abandonment at being put into care, the whole situation seemed utterly horrific. How could I possibly subject my own daughter to what would seem in her eyes to be such an obvious rejection? I tried to discuss the matter with her in order to gauge her opinion and, despite her seemingly passive demeanour, I could see her fiery hatred of me burn in her eyes as she said she didn't care one way or the other. Heidi would not let me help her pack as she prepared to leave for a foster family not too far away, and it felt as if my heart was being torn from my chest when she left without so much as a word. To me, this was confirmation that I was a complete failure as a mother. I had been unable to cope with my daughter and so she had been sent to people who were obviously better parents than I could ever hope to be.

After a short period without contact, part of the agreement drawn up by social services was for Heidi to return home for day visits. On the first few occasions, Heidi was extremely hostile and the tension was almost unbearable. Over time, however, this eased to the point where days became overnight stays, then weekends, and finally she was to come home for an entire half-term. The first weekend of this holiday was our wedding anniversary, and whilst I wasn't sure about both Dave and me going out and leaving her alone with the other children, Heidi was most insistent. Eventually, safe in the knowledge that my mum was only just over the road and would be on call to deal with any potential problems, we agreed to go out for the evening to celebrate. If anything, Heidi hinted the occasion was important to her as a chance to prove she could be trusted and, all smiles, she ushered us both out of the front door, telling us to have a great time. Nevertheless, on arriving at the Chinese restaurant, my priority was not to look at the menu but to phone home. Heidi answered promptly to assure me that Alex and Megan were fast asleep in bed and that everything was fine. Dave and I ordered our meals, but I was in no mood to linger over mine, as the uncomfortable feeling in the pit of my stomach, perhaps a mother's instinct calling me home, did little for my appetite. Neither did Dave's insistence that I was stupid to worry so much. He had remained pretty detached throughout the period when Heidi had first gone into care, and my frustration about his apparent lack of concern had only served to drive a wedge between us. He seemed so dismissive of my worries, making me feel yet again that I was a silly little woman.

There certainly seemed nothing to worry about as we pulled into the drive: the house was still standing and the downstairs lights were on. On entering, however, there was no sign of Heidi and nor did she respond to my calls. I rushed upstairs to the girls' room and inched the door open quietly so as not to alarm them, but as soon as I stepped inside in my bare feet, I could feel that the carpet was sodden underfoot. Switching on the light, I could now see vomit all over the floor and Heidi lying in an unconscious heap on her bed. I shouted down for Dave's help, and we somehow managed to shift her almost lifeless body into the bathroom, where we simultaneously cleaned her up and tried to revive her from her drunken stupor.

I left Dave to attend to Heidi whilst I checked the drinks cabinet downstairs to see the extent to which she had sampled all the spirits. It was clear she'd drunk an awful lot, but it was while stripping her bed that I was stopped dead in my tracks, for there I found a spilled bottle of paracetamol. I shuddered at the notion that Heidi might have tried to kill herself in the same manner as I had just a few years before. Frantic with worry, I phoned the hospital and then my mother to look after the other two as Dave and I dashed to A & E with Heidi. I sat in the back with her, shaking my daughter and trying to wake her up, but she barely responded, and I was struck by the sheer terror that perhaps we had discovered her too late.

The hospital staff were as swift as they were efficient, taking control of the situation as soon as we came through the main entrance. Now all I could do was put my full trust in them and hope for the best as the minutes dragged by for Dave and me in the waiting room. I was unable to judge the nurse's mood as she approached us with the news, but a huge wave of relief rolled over me and I hugged her with gratitude as she explained Heidi was going to be all right, that she had only drunk the alcohol and not taken any of the tablets, and we'd be able to take her home in a short while. Heidi was still extremely groggy on the journey back, and as soon as we got home, I took her up to my room and tucked her up in bed for the night before cleaning up the rest of the mess in her room. Whilst doing this, I found food wrapped up in little parcels under her bed, along with small bundles of cash and some clothes in a bag. It was clear to me that Heidi had been planning some form of escape for a while, whether it was to run away or commit suicide, but it was equally clear the following morning that she was not prepared to admit to this and, however much I yearned to know the truth, I was reluctant to interrogate her whilst she was in such a fragile state.

She returned to her foster parents that day, and the matter was not mentioned again. Her visits home became far less tempestuous, so the events of that night were merely swept under the carpet for fear of causing further problems. This had been a wake-up call for me, though, as the fear of losing my precious daughter helped me to focus on her problems for a while rather than my own. I started trying to rebuild the bridges between us, paying her as much attention as possible during the times when she was at home, and we even went on a camping trip together. She benefited from all the interest I was showing in her, and gradually her behaviour grew less volatile. This improvement in our relationship, however, was accompanied by the deterioration in that between Dave and me.

SEVENTEEN

Wolves in Sheep's Clothing

Although I prided myself on my ability to keep house, I had done little else with my life, moving straight from my birth-parents' house to those of my successive husbands, and I began to develop an urge for new experiences. I struck upon the idea of providing a catering service to accompany some of the functions where Dave performed, and such was the success of the initial ventures that I finally decided to take the plunge and develop my own business.

It was all very much trial and error to begin with, as I had no formal training and no business plan to speak of. There was no bank loan to help me get started, so I found other means to fund my dream, namely doing odd jobs for my neighbours, which included everything from a spot of painting to chopping their firewood for them. The cost of advertising my new service was out of the question, but I managed to overcome this particular problem by scouring the local paper for notices such as engagement announcements and then sending out a few prospective letters offering my services. Although I was starting from scratch, the years spent cooking for my family served to stand me in good stead and, as word spread, I began to receive orders for all manner of functions, from weddings and funerals to christenings and birthdays. It was hard work, but I thrived on the sense of purpose it gave me, and it also offered me the occasional opportunity to work alongside my husband, whom I hardly saw these days due to the amount of extra singing work he'd begun to take on.

The busier my business became, however, the more Dave seemed to resent it. The success I started to achieve gave me more self-confidence. I enjoyed meeting other people outside our home and thrived on the praise that I received for my work. Dave clearly felt threatened by this, as he had very clear ideas about who was in the driving seat in our marriage. He was the provider while I was supposed to be the meek little woman running his home. As I took on more work, we started to argue more and more frequently, and he accused me of neglecting him and the children for the sake of my 'little hobby', as he liked to call it. He spent increasing amounts of time away from home, claiming that he had been booked in towns further away and had to stay overnight, but I started to worry that there was more to it than that and became suspicious that he might be seeing someone behind my back.

Rather than deal with the problems in my marriage face-on, I buried my head in the sand and threw myself even further into my work. Eventually, all the effort seemed to be paying dividends. I expanded not only to cater for the clients' wishes in terms of food, table arrangements and cakes but I also organised photographs, marquees, outside bars and entertainment. I loved every minute of it, and today I would probably have been given the grand title of wedding planner. Perhaps with three marriages under my belt already I knew what I was doing!

Evenings tended to be the only times I could consult with my clients, as I usually had functions to attend to at the weekends and most clients were at work during the day. The evening consultations were invariably long, often lasting for several hours, and just as I would think that everything had been agreed, the bride, her mother or some other well-meaning person would probably throw a spanner in the works and then it would be all change.

If he wasn't out working himself, Dave would be waiting for me when I returned home from these evening sessions with 20 questions, and he would even check the mileage on my car, so convinced was he that I'd been somewhere other than I'd said. It soon reached the point where I would dread the thought of going home, as I was so scared of the confrontation that surely lay ahead, especially if I was back later than I had said I would be. During the day, he would ring home several times just to check up on me, and if I was out of the house, he would phone my mum and demand to know where I was. He seemed to resent my small successes, and if someone complimented me on the business, he would be quick to point out that I should be putting more effort into looking after him. Despite the provocation, I remained resolute in my determination to make the business a success, and I even started to look on it as a potential escape route from my increasingly unhappy marriage.

I had never had any access to Dave's bank account; he had always given me my housekeeping each week and I'd simply made ends meet. I didn't even know what his earnings were, and I had never questioned the situation. I had no savings of my own, and so the money from the business was all I would have to support me if I did decide to leave Dave. To strengthen my position, I enrolled in a small-business course at a nearby town during the day, when Mum could look after the children, and in the evenings, I studied at a book-keeping class.

This was the marriage that was supposed to have been for life, the one I was finally not going to mess up, and yet here I was once again feeling that my life was falling apart around me. My outside interests might have helped fill some of the void, but I desperately wanted to confide in someone about how unhappy I was. By this time my dad was quite poorly, so Mum already had her hands full; she didn't need any more worries, and especially not from me after all the trouble I'd caused over the years. In desperation, I turned instead to my friend and former neighbour Wendy. We'd remained in touch since my time with Sean and become much closer over the years. Wendy had troubles in her own marriage, which had been rather volatile for a while. Her husband worked away from home a lot of the time and, according to Wendy, he had been having affairs on and off for years.

With both of us seeing a trouble shared as a trouble halved, we increasingly began to cry on each other's shoulders, as friends do, and Wendy confided in me that she had been having an affair of her own with a coach driver she'd met on holiday. She didn't see him as often as she wanted to because his work took him all over Europe. There was also the problem of him being married. She described her lover in glowing terms as a big handsome man with a thick head of black hair and a winning personality to match his looks. I in turn confided in Wendy about my unhappiness and suspicions that Dave was seeing someone else. I came to rely on her more and more, and I had no qualms about telling her of my growing ambition to earn enough through my business to leave my husband and support my children.

EIGHTEEN

True Colours

I recognised Stuart's voice as soon as I picked up the receiver, but I was rather taken aback as I'd assumed it would be Dave calling to check up on me again. I was even more taken aback by what Stuart had to say. He was a young man whom I'd known for at least five years, as he was the son of the landlord at one of the pubs where Dave had a regular gig. We'd always got on very well, and now he was a little bit older, he'd begun to flirt with me occasionally. I have to admit I was rather flattered, but I never thought any more of it than that. To be told over the phone he had to see me over an urgent matter was a little disconcerting, but he sounded so insistent that I agreed to meet him later outside the hall where I was working that evening.

Once we were both sitting in my van, Stuart came straight to the point and asked me whether or not I knew that Dave had been having an affair for quite some time. It hurt to have my suspicions confirmed, but the news was hardly a shock – that was until Stuart explained that Dave wasn't seeing just one other woman but several. I asked him to try to find out more details and arranged for him to drop by the house the following week, when I knew Dave would be out.

Stuart performed his task well, for when he came to the house, he was able to tell me that Dave was almost certainly seeing one woman in the next town and another further afield. He was also, however, involved with a woman from the village. When Stuart and I had first discussed this in my van, I'd felt nothing but a hollow ache at the thought of Dave's infidelity, but to hear he was carrying on right on our own doorstep was too much to bear, and I could not help but break down and cry. By the time my husband returned home, however, I had managed to regain my composure, and he was none the wiser about my discovery. I did wonder about Stuart's motives in telling me about Dave's affairs, but as his claims only confirmed my own suspicions, I accepted what he had told me as fact.

A few weeks later, Dave told me he was planning to go away for a couple of nights, ostensibly to perform, and as the venue was some distance away he was to stay over rather than drive back each evening. Under normal circumstances, his suggestion wouldn't have been unreasonable, but now I instinctively felt his intention was to meet up with one of his lovers. Despite his own indiscretions, he maintained his paranoid jealousy towards me, and as he left for another gig that night, he told me that there was no point in thinking I could go out while he was away as he had disconnected the car battery.

This remark, on top of everything I had been told,

was the final straw. During one of my business courses, I had met a chap called Mark, who was as charming as he was tall, dark and handsome. He'd let it be known that he was interested in me, and I decided the next time he asked me to go out for a drink I would accept. I was sick of Dave's insinuations and decided if I was to be accused of having an affair, I might as well go ahead and have one.

After my class that week, Mark once again suggested that we go out for a drink, and he seemed delighted when I accepted, suggesting that we meet in a club he knew in town. When I arrived, my heart was in my mouth, but it was not with the thrill or expectation of some heady illicit romance. The whole time we spent at the club, I was convinced I would be spotted by prying eyes, and with my earlier confidence all but dissolved, I thanked Mark for the drink but told him I must go home. As I had left early, it was not late by the time I arrived home, but it was obvious Dave was the worse for wear, having in my absence indulged in his love of whisky to a large degree. He turned on me immediately, perhaps spurred on by the guilt I felt showed on my face. I had gone out with the intention of cheating on him, and while I hadn't been able to carry out my plan, I felt that he would still be able to see right through me, so I left him downstairs and went quickly to bed.

His footsteps up the stairs thudded as heavily as my heart, and I was just getting into my nightie as he burst into the room and came straight for me. In one violent motion, he grabbed me tightly by the neck and threw me onto the bed, swatting me like a fly each time I tried to get to my feet. I was no match for his physical strength, yet still I struggled against him until he ripped out the front of my nightie with such brute force he left deep, livid gouge marks down my chest. In a split second, my resistance was crushed, as all sorts of memories and emotions rushed to the front of my mind. Some I recognised clearly; others were just out of view, but in that moment I was sure I could in some way taste and smell the horrors of the past. All I could do was plead for mercy and beg him not to hurt me, but my cries were all in vain. First, he pulled me by a clump of my hair, making me feel as if it would be wrenched from its roots, and then he slapped me hard, as I urged him not to wake the children with his bellowing. With that, he forced himself upon me, and whilst rape within marriage did not exist in those days, he penetrated me against my will with all the violent aggression the act entails.

It was during this part of the ordeal that I became aware of the door opening slightly, and there in the half-light stood Alex. As best I could, I motioned to my son that all was fine, mouthing the words, 'I'm OK, go back to bed, love,' whilst Dave was so intent on what he was doing that he was not aware of a thing. When he had finished, he slumped down on top of me, exhaling his whisky-soured breath, and before long had fallen into a drunken sleep. I managed to roll him off me and fled to the bathroom. At that precise moment, I was not sure what was worse, being raped by my husband or my son seeing it happen.

I washed my face and forced on a smile before going to Alex's bedside, where the light from the streetlamp outside lit his face where he lay, illuminating his tears and terror. I innocently asked my young son what was wrong, and he replied, 'Why did Daddy hurt you?' I tried to reassure him by saying that Daddy and I had been playing; it was just a bit of 'rough house', as we used to call it, like when he and Daddy wrestled on the floor. He seemed to accept my explanation and soon fell asleep in my arms. I crawled into bed with him, leaving Dave alone in our room.

The next morning was absurd, as I struggled to maintain a pretence of normality for my children's sakes while waiting for Dave to leave the house. My only comfort was that I could see he was suffering from a really severe hangover. Once I was on my own, I was haunted by recurring images of the night before and, unable to reach Wendy on the phone all day, a part of me truly wanted to die as I struggled to deal with it all alone. Dave kept his distance from me on his return, and as the evening slipped by, with no mention made of the previous night's attack, I managed to maintain the brave face that had masked my true emotions all day.

The following morning, it really did seem like business as usual as Dave and I set off for Staffordshire to purchase some china for my business. We travelled in an awkward silence, only stopping en route for toilet breaks. Whilst Dave went off to the gents, I took the opportunity to call Wendy, but yet again I couldn't reach her. In my torment, it felt as if I were in some sort of trance, living half in the past, half in the present, and with no idea as to what the future could hold in store.

The next evening, Dave and I had a pre-arranged dinner party to host to which Wendy and her husband had been invited. I hoped this might give me the chance to talk to her, but the opportunity never presented itself. Perhaps it was all in my mind, but I had the distinct impression she had been deliberately avoiding all eye contact with me. I finally managed to get through to her by phone the following day, and I couldn't help but relay the account of the assault and rape by my husband as if I was unburdening a heavy load. Although she was not there in person to offer me support, I longed for some words of comfort, but Wendy's reply left me momentarily speechless when she said, 'Well, you looked all right to me yesterday evening. Are you sure you're not exaggerating?' I was so angry at her response, but all I could muster in reply was, 'No, of course I'm not exaggerating,' before Wendy curtly said she had to go as she had an appointment.

The phone call left me feeling I must be going crazy, for Wendy and I spoke almost every day and told each other everything. Our conversation was so out of the ordinary, I felt something must be terribly wrong – I just didn't know what. So when Dave left the house that evening, I asked my mum if she could possibly look after the children for a while before hopping into my van and driving over to Wendy's place. There was no one at home, and so I drove around aimlessly trying to clear the fog in my head.

I felt too tormented to return home to my children. I was consumed with the thought of the rape, which had brought back so many awful memories. My natural instinct for self-blame kicked in, and I convinced myself that the breakdown of yet another relationship must be my fault. I couldn't make my husband happy and had driven him into the arms of other women. My elder daughter was still in care, proving what a useless mother I was. I drove around for hours in a virtual daze until I found myself on the outskirts of Norwich, down near a bird sanctuary. There I parked the van and spent a restless night tortured by a crushing sense of failure and horrific mental images from the past.

The following morning, I tried Wendy's number once more from a phone box, but on hearing my voice she hung up immediately. I tried once more, in case we had been cut off accidentally, but there was no reply, so, with a heavy heart, I turned the van around and headed for home. At first, I thought the morning chill must have numbed my fingers as I tried to turn the key in the back-door lock, but it soon dawned on me that the key didn't fit, and when I tried the front door, my key would not work in it either. I felt utterly confused, and this only served to heighten the tension on nerves already frayed by recent events and lack of sleep. I went to my mum's to see if she knew anything, and all she could tell me was that Dave had popped over to take the children out. I explained that I couldn't get into the house, but I could see that she was far too busy looking after Dad to give this problem her full attention; she just couldn't cope with any more stress.

I drove off in my van, once again not really knowing where I was going, but on spotting a phone box I called home in the hope that my husband might tell me what was going on. I re-dialled the number over and over again for the next few hours, but on receiving no reply I finally had to give up.

The events that followed seemed to take place in a

befuddled haze, as I was still in shock from the night of the rape and the flashbacks it had dredged up from the past. In a moment of desperation, I fished Mark's number out of my purse and dialled the B & B where he was staying. I had not seen or spoken to him since the night at the club, but he agreed to meet me when I told him of the events of the past 24 hours. I desperately wanted to see my children, but I didn't even know where they were. I also needed somewhere to stay, and didn't want to worry my mum, so when Mark kindly offered to sneak me into his room at the B & B, I didn't hesitate. I made an appointment to see a solicitor the following morning and, dragging my weary bones to Mark's bed, I collapsed there in a heap as he prepared for a night in the armchair. Despite my exhaustion, however, sleep would not come. I shook uncontrollably all night long, and my chest felt as if it were pinned underneath a heavy weight suffocating the life out of me.

The next day, the solicitor was as sympathetic to my predicament as I could have hoped, but when I described what Dave had done to me, he could do no more than confirm my fears that my husband's actions were not regarded as rape under current law. Dave would have no case to answer in court. He did, however, suggest that I see a doctor about the bruises that had not yet faded and to have the scratch marks across my chest noted. With regard to the children and the house, he made it clear that I would have a difficult fight on my hands as, in the eyes of the law, I had walked out and left the children with Dave, and the house was in his name. As I made to leave, he tried to lift my despondency by giving me the details of a women's refuge that I might wish to contact if I had no intention of returning to the marital home.

My GP noted the marks on my body and also said I was suffering from shock, which was the cause of my incessant shaking. I mentioned that I'd been feeling dreadfully cold and was also having trouble with my breathing, which he informed me was the result of acute anxiety. He wrote out a prescription, but there was little more he could do to help me.

I then went to see the women's refuge as suggested, but my heart sank when I saw the state of the place. There was no way I could take my children there to live, even as a temporary stopgap. I just couldn't put them through that. There had to be another way, so first I contacted the local council and then a housing association to see if they could help with accommodation. Each time I was told that if I didn't have the children with me, I was not eligible to be allocated a house or flat. I phoned my solicitor for advice, and it was then I realised the full extent of the catch-22 situation I now found myself in: a court would not grant me custody of my children unless I had already found somewhere for us all to live.

I tried to reach Dave again and finally got him to talk to me at his work. I told him that I knew he had been having an affair and that he had no right to lock me out of the house and keep me away from my children. Unsurprisingly, he denied my allegations and said that I was the one who had left him. I was desperate to see the children, but in a terse and emotionless tone he told me I had no rights of access as I had walked out on them. It hadn't fully crossed my mind that he might deny me all access, but for the time being he held all the aces and I buckled instantly, begging him at least to let me speak to them on the telephone. He told me I was to phone back the following evening, but when I did, he refused once more to let me talk to them, even though I could hear Alex and Megan crying in the background. 'Do you see what you have done?' he barked furiously at me down the phone, to which I shouted back, 'You raped me, Dave, what did you expect me to do?' After a brief silence, he retorted, 'You'll never get the children,' and then the line went dead.

I staggered out of the phone box as if I'd been beaten senseless, and my heart was beating so fast I thought it might explode. Through the dark winter night, I spotted the lights of a lorry coming up the road and, as if guided by some distorted instinct, I stepped off the pavement in the hope that all my pain would soon cease. I felt something tug at my arm before floating down into what seemed a deep dark hole.

I came to in the shop opposite the phone box. A woman was trying to give me water to revive me whilst a man explained he had seen me in the road and caught hold of me just before I fainted. They both wanted to call an ambulance, but I refused, as I just wanted to get out of there.

I had nowhere else to go but back to Mark's room. He was waiting for me when I arrived, but I couldn't speak for crying, so he sat patiently with me for a long time until I must have fallen asleep. Although I appreciated all of Mark's acts of kindness, I knew I was not in love with him, but I didn't know how to function without a man in my life. He offered me a place to go when I was at my most vulnerable, and it was inevitable that I ended up paying him back with the only currency I now had at my disposal. Just as I had done when I ran away to London from the approved school, I traded my body for somewhere to stay.

In order to get the children back, I needed to earn enough money to afford a place of my own, but matters were further complicated by the fact that all of my catering equipment was stored at Dave's house, to which I no longer had access, and my business began to slide as I had to cancel one booking after another. Adding to the pressure was the situation with Heidi, whose behaviour had improved so much over the previous months that it had been agreed that she could come home for good that Christmas. With the holidays just weeks away, time was now of the essence if I was to keep my family together, and so I went straight to the job centre and signed on in the hope that I would find the means to fund a home for us. Initially, however, they couldn't find anything for me, and my position looked increasingly desperate as I had to prepare for the court hearing that had been set to review temporary custody of the children.

My legs felt so weak they barely supported me as I walked into the court building, but my heart leapt as I saw Wendy sitting on one of the benches, and I walked straight up to her with the intention of putting my arms around her. She spotted me, too, but as she stood up, she made no move towards me and said nothing, all the while looking over my shoulder. As I turned around, I saw Dave standing behind me, and in that awful moment, everything fell into place. It was Wendy with whom he had been having the affair; he was the 'coach driver' she had told me so much about.

It all made perfect sense now, and it had been right in front of my eyes the whole time. The remnants of my world came crashing down around me, and instead of staying to fight for my children, I found myself running from the building, sobbing uncontrollably.

While it might have been expected that this discovery about my husband's betrayal with my best friend would have made me so angry that I would have been determined to stay and confront them, I had no reserves left with which to struggle on. All I could think was that I had failed yet again. Who could blame my husband for going off with another woman when I was such a useless wife and mother? In my devastation and exhaustion, I also began to think that maybe my children would be better off without me; I didn't know how to fight Dave to get them back.

The days that followed passed in a haze of shock and pain. I couldn't believe the situation in which I now found myself and was on the verge of a complete breakdown. The misery was compounded by the fact that it was nearly Christmas, and I would not be spending it with my children. Dave got a message to me to say that I was permitted to speak to them by phone on Christmas Eve. I struggled to hide my heartbreak as I spoke to them, but this was made even more difficult by the fact that I could hear laughter and Dave and Wendy's voices in the background. It was as if I was watching the life of my family through the glass of a goldfish bowl; everything seemed the same as normal except I was on the outside.

Early in the new year of 1986, Mark and I found a small house to rent on the other side of town, and I hoped this might persuade Dave to let the children come and visit. After his initial refusal, he suddenly phoned to say that I could have them for just one night. This coincided with a weekend when Heidi was also allowed home, as the decision had been made to keep her with her foster parents until the situation between Dave and me had been resolved. The joy of being reunited with my three children was all-consuming. Mark was away, and we spent the day playing games, going to the park and reading stories before I put the younger two to bed. Heidi, now nearly 15, was delighted that Dave and I had split up, as they had never got along. I made her all kinds of promises about getting a place of my own, and it felt as though we were really communicating properly again.

The following morning, Dave arrived all too soon to pick up the younger children and bring me back down to earth, but the success of the previous day made me even more determined to work hard and find a place of our own where we could be together. It was agreed that in future I would be allowed to see the children for a few hours every other Saturday, although this had to be under Dave's supervision at his house.

These visits quickly showed Mark in a different light, as he turned out to be like most of the men in my life: nice when it suited him and not averse to raising his fists when he didn't get what he wanted. Mark was very jealous of even the little time I spent with my children and wasted no time in showing me how unhappy it made him. I don't think he had realised that he was by no means a priority in my life, and the truth stung his pride. One Saturday, after I'd seen the children and he'd spent the day drinking heavily, we had a dreadful argument that culminated in him hitting me around the head until he knocked me to the ground. Having vented his fury, he went upstairs. I later checked to make sure he had fallen asleep before creeping back downstairs and dragging the hall phone into the cupboard, from where I phoned the police. Mark had locked all the doors, and I was too frightened to climb out of a window in case I woke him by opening it, so I was in effect a prisoner in the house until the police arrived to keep guard whilst I hastily packed my few belongings and left. I was on my own, but this time I was determined I would rely on no one but myself.

My newfound resolve seemed to pay dividends, for after stints staying at a B & B and a friend's house, I finally found a little two-bedroom cottage in a village just a couple of miles away from the children. What's more, I had also managed to get a sales job and having reached my targets in the first month, I was rewarded with a company car. Things certainly seemed to be looking up, but one fly in the ointment was that Dave was quite clearly not very keen on me moving so close. Incredibly, he was still denying that he and Wendy were involved, and I can only conclude that he had to watch what he got up to if he wanted to maintain the pretence. Once I was back living closer to my old haunts, I started to find out far more than I had ever bargained for. So-called friends were now falling over themselves to tell me how my husband and my best friend had been having an affair for about two years – so all the while I'd been crying on Wendy's shoulder, she must have been relaying the information back to Dave.

However much this might have hurt, I tried not to dwell on it, as I had much to be happy about. Alex and Megan were now allowed to come and stay at the cottage when it suited Dave, and Alex would even cycle over to see me whenever he got the chance, which was wonderful. Better still, Heidi and I were getting on so well that after a few weekend visits she asked if she could come and live with me. It was so uplifting to be reunited with my eldest once more. She no longer had to fight for my attention and it felt as if we were really resolving the issues of the past. We set about turning our cottage into a home, scrubbing it from top to bottom and choosing our own personal colour schemes. Heidi wanted a red-and-white bedroom, and that's what she got. There was no one to tell us what we could or could not do, and we revelled in this freedom.

It might be said that that I revelled in it a bit too much. I became very bitter about the way that men had used and abused me in my life, and to a degree I now wanted some form of revenge. I embarked on a series of one-night stands in my bid to be the user for a change, and whilst I derived little pleasure from the casual sex itself, I found it liberating to be the one in control and calling the shots. I didn't care about how dirty I would feel afterwards. I tried to be as discreet as possible so that Heidi didn't know what was going on, but she was less than impressed when one of these one-night stands turned into something a little bit more serious, though I ended the relationship after only a few weeks.

Heidi was also less than impressed with Dave's continued denials that there was anything going on between him and Wendy and decided to confront him one weekend after being tipped off by her brother that Wendy was likely to be around. She cycled over to see him early on the Sunday morning and finding him in the kitchen making tea, she made an excuse to go upstairs, where she saw Wendy in Dave's bed reading the Sunday papers. Soon after this, I came home from work one day to find my door kicked in. Another morning I was unable to go to work because my car tyres had been slashed, and on a third occasion, my windows were broken. I confronted Dave about this, but he denied any knowledge of the incidents. I felt sure he was the culprit by the way he laughed, but the police were not interested in investigating it any further as they considered it to be merely a 'domestic'. I had to let it go, as I couldn't prove anything against him.

NINETEEN

Strangers

We hadn't been in the new cottage for long when my company expressed an interest in expanding their business down in the Bath area. I discussed the idea of a move with Heidi, who seemed keen to make a new start, but then I had to deal with the issue of my two younger children. I desperately wanted them to come with us and started to dream of us all building a new life together out of Dave's clutches. It was never going to be that straightforward, though.

When Alex and Megan came to stay at the weekend, I asked Alex how he might feel about moving to Bath with us, as I felt that the children had been through so much it had to be their decision whether or not they wanted to go with me. He didn't share the same enthusiasm as Heidi, as he was reluctant to leave his friends and football team behind. Although I could understand his reasons, I took his decision very hard and felt it confirmed my opinion of myself as a bad mother. It seemed that even the children felt they were better off with Dave.

If Alex didn't want to join us, then I couldn't take Megan either. The pair of them were so close that I felt it would be unfair to separate them. It seemed better for them to have each other, their home, friends and familiar things around them, and even if Alex had wanted to come, there was no way Dave would have let Megan go without a fight. Unless the children told me that they were desperate to be with me, I just didn't have the confidence or strength to go through another battle. I was heartbroken to leave them behind with Dave, but Wendy was now about to move in, with her children, so they had a ready-made family. I talked it over with Mum, and she said perhaps it might be better if I got settled in a new town and showed Alex and Megan that I could make a go of life on my own, in the hope that they would choose to come back to me one day.

Once the proposed expansion had been confirmed as viable, the company sent me and a colleague called Margaret down to Bath to put things into motion and to find commercial premises and accommodation. We found a three-bedroom flat above a shop that fulfilled all the criteria, and contracts were drawn up. Margaret and I got on well with each other, and after work we would treat ourselves to a quick drink to unwind.

I hadn't spotted the three men approaching us in the wine bar as we sat chatting about what we were going to do the next day, but I noticed Margaret's attention seemed to have drifted, and I turned to see what had caught her eye. The three men introduced themselves and offered to buy us a drink, but I wasn't in the slightest bit interested and declined at first. Margaret, however, was rather keen, and in moments our glasses were refreshed as the three strangers tried to make our acquaintance. They turned out to be serving in the RAF, and one of them, Douglas Hammond, seemed to be the joker in the pack. He kept telling jokes that Margaret found hilarious, but I remained aloof – not only because I wanted to concentrate on the work schedule for the following day but also because the jokes themselves were particularly bad. However, I couldn't help but overhear one of his funnier lines and, despite my best efforts, a smile spread across my face. It seemed that Douglas's persistence had paid off, as it served to break the ice, and I started to relax a bit with the help of a couple more drinks before we left to go our separate ways.

Just before we parted, the men said they would be in the same bar again in a few days' time and perhaps we might like to meet up. Margaret was certainly keen, but I didn't want to waste their time. However much I might have enjoyed the evening, a relationship was the last thing I was looking for and, besides, there was still a lot of work to do in the little time we had left before we had to leave Bath.

Despite my best intentions, the following day I found myself thinking on and off about the joker Douglas and, much to Margaret's delight but against my better judgement, we returned to the same wine bar two nights later. Douglas's wit could break down anyone's defences, and I laughed until my sides hurt during what turned out to be the most enjoyable of evenings and one I was sorry had to come to an end. Margaret and I were due to return to East Anglia the following day, and when Douglas asked for my phone number, with a promise he'd call, I gave it to him. I didn't take his number in return, however, and when the company called the next morning to say they wanted us to stay on for three further days, I had no way of contacting him.

Tired from the long journey home, I was tempted to ignore the phone that I could hear ringing as soon as I opened the door and struggled inside my cottage carrying my suitcase, but habit and curiosity got the better of me, and I was pleasantly surprised to find Douglas on the other end of the line. He admitted that he was just about to give up as he'd been trying for days with no success and had come to believe I'd given him a dud number. I explained that I had been delayed in Bath and had only just this second returned home, and we chatted easily for a while until I heard Heidi coming up the path and I said I had to go.

Heidi had been staying with a friend while I was away. I had missed her so much, and I also couldn't wait to see Alex and Megan again. They were due to come and stay at the cottage that weekend and, armed with postcards showing off Bath at its best, I secretly hoped to change Alex's mind about moving down there with me. However, not even the lure of this beautiful spa town was sufficient, and I had to accept that both he and Megan were going to stay with Dave and Wendy. Up until that point, I had intended to apply for my share of the house when my divorce came through, but if that was where the two youngest children were going to live, I could not take the roof from over their heads, even if it left me feeling beaten beyond words as far as Dave was concerned.

A couple of weeks later, I received a phone call from

Douglas to say he would be in the area and could he pop in and see me. He brought his tent and camped in the garden, and we had a great time. The children were with me that weekend, and while Heidi was quiet and reserved, I was delighted to see how the younger two took to him: he was funny and warm and kept us laughing with his irrepressible sense of humour. We kept in touch, and I looked forward to his letters and phone calls, during which he said that once Heidi and I had moved down to Bath it would be his pleasure to show us both around.

Just as it seemed that Heidi and I were all set to start our new adventure together, life threw yet another spanner in the works when Margaret, whom I was supposed to live with, decided to leave her job. I was bitterly disappointed, as the company refused to pay the extra rent on the flat or help out with Margaret's share of the deposit. We worked on commission, and I was worried that I wouldn't make enough to support Heidi and myself. The next time Douglas phoned, he could tell that something was worrying me, and I eventually blurted out the problems that I was having. I couldn't believe it when he offered to help me out, but then I became suspicious that he would be after something in return. Life had taught me that kind offers usually had a catch: surely he would want paying somehow, and I didn't play that game any more.

Douglas immediately sensed the change of tone in my voice and assured me that even if I did move to Bath and all we ever were was just friends, then that would be OK. No one had ever talked to me like that before and, although I was still reluctant to accept his offer of help, it was the first indication that Douglas really was different from all the others.

Douglas had to go away on exercises for the next fortnight, and I really missed his cheery calls, although I consoled myself with the tender words in his letters. I had never received a love-letter before, and the butterflies I had in my stomach every time I thought of him made me feel like a teenager. These were new sensations, and my feelings for him excited and frightened me in equal measure.

By the start of the summer holidays, the arrangements for the flat were finalised. It broke my heart to say goodbye to Alex and Megan, but I promised them both in a tearful farewell that I would see them again soon. Early the following morning, once Heidi and I had finished squeezing the last of our belongings into the car, we set off on the long drive, and I tried to share in her enthusiasm for the move in an attempt to numb the pain of leaving the other two behind. It seemed to do the trick for the time being, as the pair of us set about personalising our new home in much the same manner as we had the cottage. I also launched myself fully into my work, which entailed doing demonstrations of the company's products in people's homes. Most of these demonstrations were pencilled in for the evenings, so I spent the days leafleting areas in the hope of getting more appointments. It seemed my early experience of selling my birth-father's wicker baskets had finally paid dividends, as my job was indeed a success. I was able to cover the rent and some of my worries were eased. Also, once the leafleting had been done during the day, it gave Heidi and me the opportunity to enjoy each other's company, exploring the town and eating ice creams on long walks around the historic streets.

The only cloud marring that long hot summer was the phone calls to Alex and Megan, for whilst it was lovely to hear their voices and reassuring to discover they were quite happy, it was equally sickening to learn of Dave and Wendy's quite blatant ploy of attempting to buy their favour. When Dave and I had been together, he had kept me very short of spending money. The children only rarely received any gifts, and even their clothes were mostly hand-me-downs from friends and family. Now Dave was treating them to all sorts of expensive trips out during their summer holidays, and Wendy had bought them whole new wardrobes of quality clothes. They all seemed so happy together, and I felt I could not compete.

There was also little I could say about Dave and Wendy's plans to marry as soon as our divorce was finalised. Ironically, despite their affair, Dave still divorced me for adultery as I had moved in with Mark after he had locked me out of the house. He got everything his own way, as the court case to award custody had been set for the end of summer, and I didn't contest it because the children seemed so settled, and I thought it was the right thing to do by them.

As summer slipped into autumn, I felt full of pride as I looked at Heidi in her smart uniform for her first day at her new school. It had cost me a fortune, but it was worth every penny, and I marvelled at how my young daughter was growing up to be a stunning young woman who would surely be breaking a few hearts in the not too distant future. But while things had been going really well between us, the old problems were about to surface again due to my growing relationship with Douglas.

Despite the fear I felt about getting involved with another man, inside I was still the little girl who longed to be loved. After the disasters of the past, my head told me to be cautious about getting involved with Douglas, but my heart kept telling me that he was different; once again, emotion triumphed over reason. I felt things for him I had never felt for anyone else, and I began to believe I was truly in love for the first time in my life. If Douglas had to go away, my heart ached for him, and I got so excited when I knew he was coming to see me. He began staying over for a few nights each week, and as soon as Douglas and I began spending more and more time together, Heidi's behaviour declined rapidly. At the time, I couldn't understand why and was frustrated by what I saw as her unreasonable behaviour. I would later come to see, however, that she was jealous of Douglas, even though we tried to include her in all we did. She needed me all to herself and, with hindsight, regardless of my feelings for Douglas, I should have put her happiness first and foremost. Wrapped up in my own relentless quest for love, I failed my daughter yet again, as I had Alex and Megan.

On discovering Heidi had begun bunking off school, I had no choice but to confront her, but I did so on an evening when Douglas was due to come over and we were to go out for a meal with a couple we knew. Heidi stormed out of the flat as soon as I raised the subject of her truancy. She knew all too well that Douglas would be over soon, but she had not returned by the time he and the other couple arrived. All three were very understanding when I explained I would not be able to go to the restaurant as I was so worried about my daughter, and as soon as darkness fell, the two men said they would go out and look for her. I paced the flat as the hours ticked by, and my call to the police proved fruitless as they told me she hadn't been missing for long enough for them to act. Heidi finally decided to show up at three o'clock in the morning and flatly refused to tell me where she had been as she stomped her way to bed, slamming the door behind her.

The matter certainly didn't end there, though, for the following day, the landlord called to say he had received a complaint from the neighbours about the noise, not just from Heidi's outburst the previous night but also concerning loud music on numerous occasions. It turned out that after being at her new school for only two or three weeks, Heidi had already started to bunk off with her new friends. They went back to the flat, where they played loud music all day. The landlord made it clear this was a final warning; if there were any more complaints, he would have to ask me to leave.

I was mortified and worried because we had nowhere else to go. I sat Heidi down and tried to explain the seriousness of the situation, but all she could say was that she didn't care if we were evicted, and to emphasise her point she stormed off downstairs and out of the front door, slamming it so hard behind her that the glass panels shattered. From outside, she screamed obscenities at me before running off. The landlord, who was in the shop below, heard it all, and in his rightful fury he said this was positively my last warning. Douglas repaired the door, and later that day, after he'd left, Heidi finally decided to return.

Without wishing to cause another confrontation, I calmly pointed out that her outbursts had to cease or we would be made homeless, but to no avail. She began shouting at me abusively, ignoring my reminders that the landlord was still below, before turning on her music full blast. As I reached over to turn it off, she threw herself at me. Just as she was about to strike, I grabbed her hand, but in doing so, I accidentally scuffed the soft flesh underneath her eye. It did little to deter her, as she continued to fight me violently, and it took all my strength to hold her down until a kick landed squarely in my stomach and winded me, forcing me to let her go. She then said she would tell her social worker I had beaten her up, but I went straight to the phone and called her myself. We stayed out of each other's way until the social worker came to collect her the following day, by which time Heidi sported a shocking dark bruise under her eye. She returned to Dave, who was all-forgiving and lavished presents and new clothes on her, even paying for a modelling shoot. When I tried to call her, he said that she didn't want to speak to me, so, deeply hurt, I tried not to think about Heidi in the weeks that followed. I couldn't understand how she could have gone back to Dave, whom she had always hated, but as usual, I could only blame myself.

TWENTY

Until Death Us Do Part

I knew without question that I was hopelessly in love with Douglas and wanted to spend the rest of my life with him, so it was the most wonderful present I'd ever received when I accepted his engagement ring on my birthday. Organising the wedding itself, however, had its own peculiar problems. Everything had to be done via post, as Douglas was posted abroad for the next three months and only returned two days before the big day, on 20 April 1987.

I had by now changed jobs and was working as an activity organiser at a residential home, where my job was to improve the social aspect of the residents' lives. I organised trips to concerts and quiz nights in the local pub, and for one resident who had MS, I arranged a trip to Silverstone as he was into motor racing. I loved the work, as it involved putting on a happy positive face at all times, and along with the other masks I'd developed over the years to hide my emotions, this one suited me fine. The residents certainly seemed to appreciate it, as they accepted me as a part of their one big happy family, and when I was asked whether I would like to hold our wedding reception at the home, I jumped at the chance. With the help of the cook, three of the residents even made our wedding cake, and all of them clubbed together to buy us a washing machine. This proved to be a must-have when my husband returned home from exercises with a uniform that pretty much marched itself to the washing basket!

The day itself was beautiful, and Douglas's family travelled all the way from Lancashire and Yorkshire to be there. No one from my family attended, however, as I had let a rift grow between my mum and me. I was ashamed of all the worry and distress I had caused her and my dad over the years, and part of me was also embarrassed to be embarking on my fourth marriage at the age of only 31. I was upset that none of my children were present, but no one, with perhaps the exception of Douglas, would have guessed there was any sadness behind my smile. The protective 'wall' I'd built around myself was by now so high that I could barely see over the top. Thankfully, Douglas would later prove himself to be my 'ladder'.

The RAF had allocated us a house, which I'd moved into the week before, and I adjusted pretty quickly to living on a forces' camp. I only wished, as ever, that my children were with me, without all the complications. Dave allowed us to see them on his terms, but I couldn't help but notice that he would still try to unsettle the situation at every opportunity. Douglas and I didn't have much money, and it was frustrating to buy them clothes only to find on the next visit that they had shrunk or been thrown away as they were 'unsuitable'. I also started to notice that whilst Megan was always impeccably dressed, Alex was not so fortunate, often wearing trousers that ended halfway up his legs or shoes with holes in them. It was indicative of Dave's favouritism towards his 'true' daughter, Megan. She was his special little girl, while Alex, his stepson, was left with cast-offs.

Four months after the wedding, the adventure of my married life truly began as Douglas was posted to Germany for nine months, after which the plan was for us to return for him to start a course at Brize Norton. Never having been abroad before, other than on a day trip to France on a booze run, the thought of living in Germany was particularly daunting. However, I soon discovered my fears were unfounded, as we were stationed in a town near the Möhnesee Dam, famous after being almost completely destroyed by a bouncing bomb during the Second World War, and I would come to love the beautiful surrounding countryside. Our flat was nestled within the local community at the edge of a vast forest, and we would wake to the sounds of logs being sawn and the intoxicating aroma of fresh pine. Our German was sketchy at best, so we took our trusty phrasebook everywhere, and the well-thumbed pages got an airing when I took Douglas out to a local restaurant to celebrate his birthday. We enjoyed a wonderful meal, and when we bumped into a neighbour on our return home, I asked if she had the recipe for the delicious soup we'd enjoyed. 'Oh dear,' she replied once I'd read the word from the phrasebook, 'I don't think you would want to cook that.' Puzzled by her response, I pressed her to explain, only to discover the vegetable soup had not, as we'd assumed, been full of large woodland mushrooms. We had instead savoured bowlfuls of slug soup!

Dave did not allow the children to visit us at Christmas, but they did fly over for the Easter holidays, and we had a wonderful time sliding on snow mats and sipping hot mugs of drinking chocolate, listening to the Hamlyn clock's chimes and eating giant ice creams with pears smothered in chocolate sauce at a street café. The two weeks we spent together passed all too quickly, though, and at the end of their visit, I was inconsolable for days before adding another brick to my protective wall.

Heidi by this stage was 16 and, having fallen out with Dave once more, was moving around between friends before getting a bedsit of her own. There was little contact between us for a while, as she was still very angry with me, and I was still smarting from her rejection. Eventually, though, she did come out to stay with us for a couple of weeks, and the visit seemed to go well. On her return to England, however, I received a call from Dave saying she didn't want to see or talk to me, which left me very confused. Furthermore, out of the blue I then received a letter from her saying I was no longer her mother, she never wanted to see me again, and she wished that I was dead. I was deeply hurt by her cruel words and could not fathom what had inspired them, but rather than try to get to the bottom of what was going on, I opted to swallow down my pain and add it to all the rest. To complicate this volatile mother-and-daughter relationship further, Heidi made contact with us on our return to England in the summer as if nothing had happened. She had moved away to Weston-super-Mare to live with her boyfriend, and when that relationship ended, Douglas and I would drive down from Brize Norton to see her with boxes of food just to help her out. She had an assortment of short-term jobs, such as chambermaiding and waitressing, but when she wasn't working we spent a lot of time together, and I felt as if I was getting my daughter back again. We would go window shopping in Weston-super-Mare together or share a bag of chips on the seafront, just watching the world go by.

Christmas that year afforded me an unexpected bonus when Dave allowed Alex and Megan to come and stay from Boxing Day until New Year. We picked them up early in the morning along with some of their unopened presents and drove back to Brize Norton in high spirits, although I spotted that Megan had some concern over her gifts. That evening, I asked her what was troubling her, and she explained that her dad and Wendy always gave her nice presents, gifts she had specifically asked for, yet Alex always received something horrid he didn't want. She found this hard to cope with, as she loved her brother very much and hated to see the hurt this caused him. I was so proud of her when Megan said she wanted her brother to have all the presents from us to make it fair, but the whole situation spoke volumes as to how Alex was treated at home.

Megan was not without problems of her own, as I soon discovered. She had real difficulties at night, getting upset at the very thought of going to bed and coming back downstairs to join us or climbing into our bed so she was not alone. I didn't want to make an issue of it, but she also wet the bed on the night before she was due to go home. Megan told me Wendy and Dad were fighting a lot, she could hear them through the bedroom wall and it made her cry, so I guessed she associated bedtime with arguments and this made her fearful.

I had not seen my own mum and dad since the day I'd left to live in Bath, and I would soon regret the gulf that had grown between us. I was aware Dad's health had been bad for a while, and the following Easter, whilst Douglas was on leave and we were dividing our time between relatives throughout England, we drove to East Anglia to see them for the day. It was a stopping-off point of sorts during one of our trips north, and we promised to pop in to see them again on the return trip a few days later. As we made to leave, I vividly remember my dad staring deeply into my eyes as I bent to kiss him and his telling me in an emotional voice that he loved me very much. I was a little taken aback, as I knew Dad loved me but he wasn't the sort of person to say so. As I reached the sitting-room door, I turned to look at him as he sat forward in his favourite chair. Our eyes locked for what seemed an age, and in that moment I somehow knew I would never see him again.

I was sitting on the sofa in my mother-in-law's house when the call from Robert's wife Karen came to say that Jack — she never referred to him as my dad, for in her eyes he wasn't — was dead. I was numbed with grief, and I recall nothing of the long drive back the following morning other than my last vision of Dad sitting forward in his seat to tell me he loved me in his gruff cockney accent. There was nothing Douglas and I could do with regard to organising the funeral, as Robert and Karen had it all in hand. My brother simply warned me to try not to get too emotional, as it would only upset Mum, who was struggling to cope with her loss. He had no need to warn me, as the tears would not come until Douglas and I returned home that night, when they came in floods from the deepest, darkest recesses of my being. My one consolation was that, some months before, I'd written to Dad, telling him how much I loved him and asking him to forgive me for all the hurt I'd caused over the years. He never spoke of the letter to me, but Mum later told me he'd had tears in his eyes when he read it.

We returned for the funeral, but I felt totally isolated as people were crying and trying to console my mum and brother, yet I could hear a voice within screaming, 'He was my dad, too.' He was the only one who had ever loved me as a father should, and my only way of coping with the loss was to bury it deeply within me and put my 'happy' mask back in place.

With Douglas having passed his course, we were due to be posted back to Germany again, this time to the town of Wildenrath near the Dutch border. To my surprise and delight, Dave agreed that the children could come and stay for the whole of the summer holidays, so it was with great pride we arrived at our new flat in Germany as a family, and what followed was a wonderful summer filled with laughter and fun for us all. I only wished that Heidi could have joined us, but she was now over 18, and the RAF would not allow non-dependants to move abroad with the family.

The children loved the camping expeditions down

in the Mosel Valley, where the air, particularly in late summer and early autumn, smelt sweet with the heady perfume of grapes on the vine. Megan also celebrated her eighth birthday with us, the first one we'd shared since she was four, and we all enjoyed a big party. The six weeks flew by far too quickly for my liking, and I must confess that after they left I started drinking far more than I should for a while. I pretended it was merely because the alcohol was cheaper than tea or coffee, which was true, but deep down I knew that was not the reason; I simply found it to be a convenient way to numb my heartache. Thankfully, however, Douglas spotted what was going on, and I was able to stop this habit before it developed into a problem.

From the letters I received from my youngest two, it seemed Wendy and Dave were now arguing constantly, and this anger was spilling over to affect the children. Alex was targeted, as he'd started to express his resentment of Wendy, but in Dave's eyes, Alex was so much like me as a person he was easy to bully. It reached the point where Alex was begging me in his letters to let him live with me in Germany, and although Dave initially refused to allow this, he eventually yielded.

We welcomed Alex into our home with open arms, but at the same time it broke both our hearts that Megan was now left behind on her own. They had always been very close and had relied upon each other during difficult times. Megan still came to visit us on holidays, but Dave steadfastly refused to let such a move become permanent. This resulted in Megan's behaviour deteriorating both at school and at home, to the point at which Wendy finally became too exasperated to tolerate her and, out of the blue, Dave called to say she could live with Douglas and me. When I came off the phone, it was as if I needed to pinch myself, for, with the exception of Heidi, finally my children would be with me again.

The transition period for Megan was by no means easy. She was quite clingy and needed constant reassurance, and bedtimes were still a problem as she would often ask me to lie on her bed holding her hand until she fell asleep, but the bed-wetting now occurred only on the nights before she returned to see her father on visits. I also noted how quickly Megan became adept at playing her two sets of parents and step-parents off against each other, which was only to be expected for a child in her position, and due to my guilt about having abandoned her at such a young age, I did not have the heart to correct this. Little could I have guessed the fine balancing act that is parenthood would be a skill one of my own children would soon have to learn.

TWENTY-ONE

Truth Will Out

Douglas looked at me quizzically as I put down the phone, for he knew through experience that my conversations with Heidi were as unpredictable as the weather and could cause joy or despair in equal measure. Usually he could judge my mood afterwards, but this time he seemed unable to read my wide-eyed expression, so, to answer his silent question, I simply threw my arms around him and told him Heidi was expecting a baby.

In October 1992, Heidi gave birth to little James, and he was beautiful in every way. When I first held him in my arms, I was proud enough to burst. Heidi invited Douglas and me to stay with her and her boyfriend Martin when James was just three months old. It was wonderful to see her with her child, and we seemed to form a stronger bond ourselves during our stay.

Around this time, I first began to suffer the first symptoms of a debilitating condition that would take several doctors and as many years to be properly diagnosed as fibromyalgia, a chronic condition that causes extreme pain in the muscles and joints as well as severe exhaustion, and more often than not these symptoms lead to depression. At first, I could not even pronounce the word, but having been informed that there was little that could be done in practical terms and that I simply had to learn how to manage a condition that left me feeling as if my muscles were being pulled from my very bones, I knew I had to find out more. Out of necessity, I got to learn everything I could about fibromyalgia over the next few years, until, with the aid of various detoxifying diets, acupuncture and massage, I finally reached the stage where I had control of the condition rather than it controlling me. However, the onset of my fibromyalgia was significant for another reason, and it was all thanks to the wonderfully intuitive doctor who examined me. To put me at my ease, she began chatting about anything and everything, and during the course of the conversation I somehow came to find myself talking about how much I missed my dad, and from there I started to reveal other parts of my personal life piece by piece.

Rightly suspecting she had only scratched the surface of my life story, the doctor suggested I might wish to speak further with a psychiatric nurse. Although I had my reservations about discussing my past with a man, I would soon come to realise I had nothing to fear as psychiatric nurse Steven Adams guided me through our sessions. For the very first time in my life, I started to open up in detail about what Ronald had subjected me to as a child. I found myself revealing incidents and ordeals I had kept hidden for so long, and he helped me make some sense of it all. Throughout my life, it seems that each time I suffered an ordeal I subconsciously forged a new 'mask' behind which to hide my true feelings. By the time I met Steven Adams, I had half a dozen or more of these masks of various thicknesses, each one hiding yet another unresolved emotional turmoil. With Steve's help, I'd managed to peel back a number of these masks to recognise the issues within, and now what I had to learn was how to live without the masks I had discarded. Steve suggested I read a book called *Rescuing the Inner Child* by Penny Parks, and I cannot recommend it highly enough, as it made me aware that my childhood abuse and its repercussions were by no means unique to me.

Although the notion wasn't fully formed, at this point I was also becoming vaguely aware of how the effects of my childhood traumas were not confined to me alone. The actions of my birth-father could be likened to a pebble being thrown into a pond, the concentric ripples it caused stretching far and wide.

One area in which it seemed the past was recurring in the present was in the lives of my children. Heidi's relationship with James's father had broken down. According to Heidi, he had not only cheated on her but also physically assaulted her on occasions. Douglas and I returned to England to help her move out to a B & B, but she was very unhappy there. After our return to Germany, we sent her a ticket so that she could come and stay with us for a few weeks. During her trip, she struck up a friendship with a friend of ours called Nat, and after her return to England, when she found she had been allocated a council flat, Nat began travelling back to see her whenever he could. Each time he would load up his car with gifts for Heidi and James, and it was obvious he was smitten by her. Heidi confessed to me she had strong feelings for Nat, too, and by the end of the year not only were they married and now living in Germany together, they were also expecting their first child.

Despite the whirlwind nature of their romance, I was aware not all was as rosy as it appeared, for Nat had told me Heidi was still prone to erupting into terrible rages for no apparent reason, and when they occurred, Nat felt he didn't even know who his wife was. It was put down to hormonal changes because of the pregnancy, but I began to suspect otherwise.

Alex was by now attending police college, and on the surface he seemed to be doing well, but I was concerned about him and became convinced that he was using drugs of some sort on a regular basis. Why I should suspect this, I don't know, for my knowledge of drugs was limited at best, but in time my suspicions would be proved correct.

To complicate matters, Douglas received his next posting, and we were to be sent to Cyprus for the next two years. This caused me all sorts of worries, as it was much further afield than anywhere I had been before and I didn't know what to expect. I had also become very used to having Heidi living nearby and seeing them all nearly every day. James was walking now and growing so fast, whilst Heidi and Nat's baby was due in the summer, and we would not be able to be as involved living so far away.

Douglas had a job to do, though, and this is the lot of a forces' wife, which I had known when I married him. Furthermore, Nat and Heidi could also be posted anywhere, as could Alex when he completed his police training. At least I still had Megan with me, and after consulting her school, it was decided she would come with us. As long as her schoolwork didn't suffer, it would be a good opportunity for her to broaden her horizons. We went back to England for some leave before departing for the Mediterranean and visited our families to say our goodbyes, with many tears shed by all.

On arriving in Cyprus, we were all stunned by the vast blue sky above us and by the heat. We were shown to our little two-bedroom home in a village outside Nicosia, and I was pleasantly surprised to find it kitted out with everything we needed. What's more, our personal items had been shipped from Germany some weeks earlier, so we wasted no time in turning our new house into a home before going off to explore our surroundings. We settled in very quickly, and our happiness was complete when we received the news in our first year that Heidi had given birth to a beautiful baby daughter called Lucy, whom I met for the first time when I flew home to attend Alex's passing-out parade. However, despite his achievement, Alex's life was about to come off the rails, for he was, as I'd feared, becoming hooked on drugs.

As so often tends to be the case with drug use, once the initial thrill of a high becomes commonplace, the user goes in search of something new, and Alex would prove to be no exception as he supplemented his cannabis consumption with Ecstasy. He was always honest with me about what was happening in his life, and I tried so hard to deter him from treading this path, but he was convinced he was doing nothing wrong, whereas I felt I was losing my son. Eventually, after three years' service, Alex became increasingly disillusioned with the police and decided he wanted to get out. Ultimately, however, the decision was taken out of his hands, as just weeks before he was due to leave, he was caught with some drugs on him at work. He was asked to leave the service under a cloud, a situation that would hang over him for some time to come and push him further down the slippery slope he was already on.

My health at the time continued to cause me problems, as I had not conquered my fibromyalgia by then and was often left exhausted and in pain. Most days I could not even find the energy to get out of bed, or if I did, the best I could hope for was to get washed before slumping down in a darkened room and nodding off occasionally, which interfered with my night-time sleeping pattern. To compound the problem, Megan was becoming increasingly unruly and disobedient. I feared a repeat of Heidi's behaviour, and I did not think I would be able to cope. No matter what we asked of her, she pretty much refused and seemed to go out of her way to cause trouble. Some of it could be expected from an adolescent, but I was sure much of it was fuelled by her attitude towards Douglas, Dave, Wendy, me and all that had gone on between us. Circumstances were about to conspire to make matters a whole lot worse.

Up until my illness struck, I had always had my own job and had never asked Dave for any maintenance. Now, however, I was unable to work, and when he refused my request for help, I had no choice but to contact the Child Support Agency. He did his best to avoid them, but they eventually presented him with a demand for a few thousand pounds. Douglas and I had never wanted this to happen and felt the CSA were asking for too much, but Dave had left us with little choice.

His reaction, however, was inexcusable, as he wrote to Megan claiming that he would have to sell his house to meet the demand. He stated that this had been my real intention all along, and he would commit suicide before he let that happen. I may have hated Dave, but I would never have stooped so low, and the effect of his letter on Megan, now in her early teens, was immediate. From being difficult, she became completely out of control: we seldom knew where she was or with whom. She would sneak out of her window late at night while we were asleep to meet up with some very undesirable people, and tales were coming back to us that she was putting herself in dangerous positions with both boys and young soldiers. Ultimately, I couldn't cope with the guilt trip Dave had foisted upon Megan, so at the eleventh hour I stopped the action. Dave agreed to pay money to us at a lesser rate, although he sent it straight to Megan, who then frittered it away on cigarettes and other treats for her friends. If we complained, she would argue that her dad had told her the money was hers, not ours, and it was none of our business, further undermining our relationship with her.

Matters came to a head during a blazing row when Megan stated she wanted to return to her father. Once tempers had cooled, she still insisted that this was her wish, and Douglas and I were so tired of fighting with her that we gave in to her demand, though it was certainly not what we would have wanted.

The main highlight of this difficult year was receiving news from Heidi that she was expecting her third child in the autumn, and although this scuppered any hopes we had that Heidi and her family would come to visit us soon, I was thrilled to hear in the November that baby Thomas had made his entrance into the world. I could not wait to return home to see him.

My joys were, however, fleeting these days, as I increasingly found myself dwelling on past events that, at my lower points, left me consumed with guilt and shame. These lows crept up on me without warning and, as I sank into depression, I continued my now well-established pattern of placing the blame for everything that had gone wrong in my life, and subsequently my children's lives, firmly at my door. I tried to focus on our impending return to England, but Cyprus held one last surprise in store before we packed our bags.

TWENTY-TWO

The Long Journey Back

I eyed the airmail letter in my hand curiously, for although the British postmark and stamps were familiar, the handwriting on the envelope was not. It turned out to be a letter from a couple I didn't know called Tom and Carol, and sitting down to read I learnt they had managed to track me down to Cyprus via my mum. It seemed they were both volunteers at a home for the elderly in Truro, the very home where my birth-parents now lived.

Such contact out of the blue was a real shock, as well over ten years had now passed since I'd last seen Emily and Ronald. But on re-reading the pages, my initial surprise and confusion gave way to curiosity, and I accepted their kind offer of help in contacting my birth-mother. Over the coming months, I was at last able to forge some kind of relationship with her, Emily dictating her letters to Tom and Carol, while they helped her to read out the ones I sent to her in return. There were so many questions I wanted to ask her, mainly about why she had stood by and not protected me from Ronald, but I couldn't bear the thought of strangers reading this out to her, and so I restricted myself to telling her all my news about the children and about my life with Douglas.

Ronald was by now completely blind as well as deaf, and it gave me a sense of comfort to read that for the first time in over 40 years of married life Emily was now in a position to do as she wished without fear of him finding out. He had finally lost his control over her, and she apparently expressed this new-found freedom by treating herself to whatever expensive jewellery and new clothes took her fancy. Emily also expressed a wish to see me and the children, and I was touched to discover she still had the small photo album with our pictures inside that I had given her on our last meeting all those years ago.

Douglas and I were due to return to England in May and, unbeknown to Ronald, a secret family reunion with Emily was planned for our return. In the meantime, I embroidered a bird in a cage entwined with flowers, a poignant reminder of all the times Emily had been prevented from teaching me to sew. I wanted to show her I had indeed managed to master the craft so that she would be proud of me, and I framed it ready to send to her for her birthday just a few weeks before we were due to meet.

The day before Emily's birthday, I answered the phone to hear my brother Robert's voice on the line. My pleasure at this surprise was short-lived, as he told me Emily had been rushed to hospital and the situation didn't look good. The news stunned me, and the receiver slipped from my fingers as I slumped to the floor, aware only of a low anguished groan emanating from somewhere deep inside me. I knew instinctively that my birth-mother was dying.

Somehow I managed to phone Douglas, and within a few hours, arrangements were made for me to fly back to the UK. But as I boarded the small helicopter to take me to Nicosia, I momentarily felt as if the air had been sucked out of my lungs, and I knew then I'd felt Emily go. I tried to convince myself otherwise, but in my heart I knew I was too late. The long flight to London was little more than a blur, and as I made to leave the plane at Heathrow, I was met by a member of the RAF, who confirmed what I already knew: that Emily had died at the very moment I'd boarded the helicopter.

On hearing the news, I had to suppress the urge to scream. I felt robbed, as the opportunity finally to have some sort of meaningful relationship with my birth-mother had been cruelly snatched from me just as it had seemed it might happen. All chance of reconciliation was gone, and all my many questions would now go unanswered. I was simultaneously racked with confusion as to why I should feel such grief over the loss of someone who had been so distant in my life, someone who had not protected me when I needed it the most, who had played along with Ronald and hurt me as per his instructions. Deep down, however, I already knew the answer to this: she'd never been in a position to love and protect me as I'd needed her to, as she was as much a victim of his as I was. At least now she was free, and I wished her peace.

When I reached the hospital, I was taken to the mortuary to view her body. Once in the room, I broke down into racking sobs, and all I could do was take her in my arms and hold her, rocking her back and forth, trying to comfort us both. I wanted to tell her that everything was OK: that I forgave her and knew how difficult life had been for her.

Ronald was in the dining room when I went to the home to sort out Emily's belongings, and I slipped into what had been their room as quickly as I could. Carol and Tom accompanied me, and I don't know how I would have coped without their help. As soon as I opened the wardrobe, silent tears streamed down my face, as there on a hanger I spotted what was obviously a well-worn and favourite hand-knitted cardigan. Ronald would never allow his wife to buy all the wool she needed for the knitting she loved so much, so she was forced to buy balls of different types, colours and thicknesses. With these odd collections, she would knit jumpers and cardigans of bright, assorted colours. I gently took down the cardigan from its hanger and wrapped its arms around me, imagining she was still inside it, as I could still smell from the wool the scent of the violet water she'd always worn. By the window stood a tapestry frame in which the needle lay still threaded, awaiting her nimble fingers, and in the cupboard by her bed I discovered Emily's wedding album, two further albums full of pictures of her childhood, images of me as a small child and pictures of my three children alongside the postcards and letters I had sent to her over the past year. Was it possible that Emily really had always loved me in her own way after all?

I met with the head of the home, who treated me in a

polite but frosty manner. I could tell she did not approve of me, and I could see in her face that she believed I had simply abandoned my poor disabled parents. However, she did not object to us having a tea at the home after the funeral service or to my request for a rose tree to be planted in Emily's memory in the garden. My birth-mother might now be gone, but I did not want her forgotten, and the home seemed the most appropriate place, as it was there she had finally found a degree of happiness at the end of her life.

The funeral itself promised to be an emotional roller coaster, and I asked for Ronald not to be made aware of my presence. I could not have borne to touch him in any way, or for him to have touched me. Just before the service, I sat with Emily for the last few fleeting moments we would spend together. I placed three flowers in her coffin, one from each of her grandchildren, the little picture I had sewn for her birthday and a photograph of us all, including the great-grandchildren she'd never met, as I did not want her to be on her own any more. I talked to her about us all and told her I now knew that what had happened during my childhood wasn't her fault. I finally believed she would have saved me if she could. I only wished she could have saved herself and had a better life with someone who loved her in return.

As we walked towards the crematorium, a familiar voice momentarily stopped me in my tracks and sent a shiver down my spine. Ronald's guttural tones filled me with the same sense of all-consuming dread they had so many years ago, and again I felt my legs go weak. I could see him now with someone on either side of him helping him into the building, and as I walked inside, I peered apprehensively towards where he sat at the front before taking a seat next to my mum two rows behind. Once the service began, I couldn't see through my tears or hold my hymn book still, and my distress wasn't caused solely by the loss of Emily but also because I was so close to this man who had so brutally stolen my childhood and innocence.

Afterwards, the congregation made its way back to the home and upstairs to a little room for refreshments. Ronald sat alone in an armchair, and everyone else sat or stood around rather awkwardly. I stifled a reaction as I overheard Robert's partner Karen comment on what a nice old man Ronald seemed to be, for she could never have guessed what kind of monster once lurked within the frame of this sweet little vulnerable-looking old man. She had no knowledge of how this same person would creep into my bed night after night to force himself inside me, how at bath-times he would scrub my private parts until I bled or how he made me shake with fear at the prospect of the next physical attack as I sat perched precariously on aching knees before him for hours on end reading the Bible. Yet in that same moment, I suddenly saw Ronald for what he had truly become, a pathetic shell of a man of whom I no longer had any need to be afraid.

After the funeral tea was over, one of the nurses gave me a white toy cat, a present they had given to Emily the previous Christmas and something she kept with her until the day she died. As I held it, I could almost imagine I felt it vibrate with her energy. I held on to it all the way back to Cyprus, and it is something that I've kept to this day. It is all I have left as a semblance of something I never had but always craved: my very own mother's love.

As planned, Douglas and I returned to England in 1996, eventually buying our first home there, a modest semi in High Wycombe. Whilst I may have had little schooling under my belt, and none from the age of 13 onwards, I still possessed the will to work hard and turn a house into a home, which is exactly what Douglas and I proceeded to do. However, my health still remained an issue. My fibromyalgia may have been kept in check, but it was not cured, and now I started to suffer badly due to the damage my body had sustained from falling through the window at the approved school. I had constant problems with my ankle and knees, and my wrists had also been damaged, as I'd landed in a crouching position. When I went for treatment, eventually undergoing a series of operations, I had to explain how I had sustained the original injuries, and the physical pain I was suffering was matched by the emotional torment I felt at dredging up all these bad memories from the past.

I had long suffered from disturbing flashbacks, but they now seemed to increase not only in frequency but also in their graphic nature. These vivid nightmares were starting to pose an ever-increasing problem within my marriage, as I became physically and emotionally withdrawn, and Douglas grew frustrated at his inability to reach me and help me. I knew I loved Douglas, but I was finding it more and more difficult to express this to him, and I was terrified that I would lose him.

In an attempt to address my issues, I started to explore alternative therapies such as Reiki, and I studied for a diploma in stress management as well as taking a counselling course, with the prospect of doing voluntary work with survivors of abuse. I think deep down I knew I still had a lot of personal issues to resolve before I was in a position to help others, but nevertheless I learnt a great deal about myself during this period. One topic that came up was boundaries, as children who have been abused seldom grow up to recognise any, with obvious consequences. In a relationship between a parent and child, each has their own role to play. A parent is supposed to teach the child what is acceptable behaviour and also the consequences of unacceptable behaviour. In an abuse situation, however, the child learns a warped set of rules about what is acceptable physical behaviour and carries that with them into every future relationship. I also learnt how to express my feelings with greater clarity, and about total trust, the latter achieved by being led blindfolded through an assault course with only my sighted partner's guidance there to keep me safe.

Safe and positive methods of expressing anger and pain were also taught, such as punching pillows or drawing pictures and then venting any anger or pain by tearing them up, but perhaps the most challenging part of the course for me was acknowledging the past and identifying its role in my future.

As I felt my confidence grow, I decided I wanted to take an evening class, although I was at a loss as to what I would study. I picked up a booklet from my local supermarket on forthcoming local classes, and while flicking through the pages, I came across a course on sign language. I stared at the information before me with mixed emotions. The deaf world was certainly not a place that held any fond memories for me, so initially I dismissed it and concentrated on the information about other available courses. For some reason, however, I felt compelled to return to the page on sign-language lessons. I could still vaguely remember some of what I had learnt as a child to communicate with my birth-parents and, having talked it over with Douglas, I decided that I would give it a go. What I couldn't understand was why I felt so compelled to do so.

Attending that first class of the autumn term was particularly daunting. I have never been a very confident person, regardless of the impression I might give to others, but with each passing lesson, I realised to my amazement that I remembered much more than I had at first thought possible. As my knowledge grew, so did my self-belief. I found that not only did I have a real vocation for signing, I also loved to perform it, and it wasn't long before I had passed my first examination. I also managed to get a part-time job with an association for the blind as a communicator guide, working with people who had partial hearing and sight. This served to get me back into the workplace, but I also found I really loved my job and had a deeper understanding for it than I could ever have imagined.

For my Guild Communication qualification, I was sent away on a number of courses, during which I learnt a lot about Ronald's condition, retinitis pigmentosa. This helped me to understand a little better how difficult it had been for him and perhaps why he had been so frustrated and bitter with the world. I also learnt how to communicate with people who were not only deaf but blind as well and, although I hadn't consciously realised it at the time, I had now acquired the skills to communicate with Ronald.

I met many wonderful people from all over the South and the Midlands during the course of my studies. One day, after I had been there for a number of weeks, I happened to overhear a woman talking about someone called 'Ronnie'. My heart raced, as intuitively I knew she must be talking about Ronald. Without revealing to her what my connection to this man might be, I began asking the woman some vague and innocuous questions about him. It soon became apparent we were indeed talking about my birth-father, and I learnt that the woman was a voluntary care worker in the residential home where he now lived.

I'd had no contact with Ronald since Emily's death. The only part he played in my life now was as part of the past I tried to suppress, but on hearing his name, I suddenly felt inexplicably driven to track him down.

After several weeks, I finally managed to trace the social worker who had been assigned to Ronald and Emily just before her death. I told her a little bit about my past and the reasons why I had not been in contact with my birth-parents for a number of years. Then I explained my need to see Ronald. I didn't wish to harm him, but I needed to put some ghosts to rest, and she seemed to understand, giving me details of the home to which he had now been moved. The head of the home was rather reluctant at first to agree to my proposed meeting with Ronald, as he was in her charge and she didn't want him upset. I fully appreciated this but stressed my need to try to sort things out before it was too late for both of us, and we agreed that we would leave the decision to him. She explained that Ronald was by now a very frail old man suffering a lot of pain from an ulcerated mouth that he would not allow anyone to look at, so I was not hopeful of the meeting taking place. To my surprise, though, just two days later the woman phoned back to say he wanted to see me. I immediately felt my hand begin to tremble as I struggled to replace the receiver.

On the morning of the trip, I dressed carefully, obviously not for Ronald, as he wouldn't be able to see me, but for my own confidence, as it made me feel I was slightly more in control of the situation. Even so, I was far from at ease, and I asked my friend Caroline to accompany me. I struggled to keep my composure as we approached the entrance to the home and, glancing around the lounge area, my heart seemed momentarily to stop as I spotted Ronald. He seemed to have shrunk in size even in the time following Emily's funeral, and for a moment I questioned my intentions. Then I heard his voice, and all of those familiar fears instantly came flooding back. I remembered all the times I had been unable to defend myself and say 'no'. Now I had the chance to set the record straight, to confront him about what he had done to me.

We were led into Ronald's room and waited for a member of staff to guide him in. He sat in the chair next to me, with Caroline sitting opposite, and I scanned his face as he stared blankly in front. I knew I had to take his hand to begin to communicate with him, but the mere thought of this caused any semblance of bravery to vanish, and suddenly I was just a frightened little girl again. However, I knew this might be my last chance, so somehow I summoned up the courage to reach out. Just the sensation of his familiar hand in mine made me feel sick, but this time it wasn't hurting me, punching me or touching me; it just waited for me to speak.

One method of communicating with someone who is deaf-blind is to spell out each word on the hand using a slightly different alphabet from the standard deaf one. I needed the whole of Ronald's hand open to speak with him, but as the minutes passed by, he kept his fingers slightly curled. Nevertheless, I began by spelling my name, and at first the hand remained still. Then Ronald suddenly squeezed my hand in a secure grip, tugging me towards him then pushing me away. Backwards and forwards he pushed and pulled me: it was as if he didn't want to hear what I wanted to say but neither did he want me to go. Gradually, bit by bit over what seemed an eternity, I managed to tell him a little about my life, that I had a good job and a happy marriage with children and grandchildren.

Then I proceeded to tell him that he and I both knew what had happened all those years ago, that he had been wrong to do those things to me and that in spite of it all I had survived. I was a good person and he had not broken me.

Ronald's mouth took on that same evil twist I remembered so clearly from my childhood. When his lips drew back, I could see nothing but black teeth lining his gums, and he looked every bit the monster I remembered. He continued to push and pull my hand backwards and forwards, but as each word was spelt out to him, piece by piece, I felt myself taking back control of my life. In that moment, I wondered who the victim had been – Me? Him? Both of us? – just where and what did his all-consuming hatred stem from? I began to feel sorry for him, as I was now able to walk away and make the most of my life, but he would remain trapped in the past, for that was all he had left and there was no way he could escape his mind.

At no point during the visit did Ronald attempt to say anything to me. At the end, I wished him well and told him I would not return, as I had said all I needed to say. As I went to pass him, I reached down and kissed the top of his head, not out of pity but because I now felt in a position where I could show him the compassion he had never shown to me. Finally, my life was changing for the better. It would still be a long and more painful journey than I could imagine, but I felt as if I had taken the first steps and was moving forward.

TWENTY-THREE

The Catalyst

If I hadn't seen the punch coming, she would have hit me straight in the face, but instinctively I pulled my shoulders in, ducked and turned my head to the side so the force of the blow connected with my ear. There was a sickening thud, sending shockwaves of pain throughout my skull, and I staggered in a disorientated fashion as I struggled to regain my balance. All I could do was try to stay on my feet in order to protect myself from this onslaught, for I knew if I went to the floor I would stand no chance. My assailant grabbed a handful of my hair and yanked my face towards her own as she spat a further torrent of vitriolic abuse at me. Then the kicks and punches resumed. I could vaguely make out Megan's voice in the background, phoning for the police, and I could only hope and pray that someone would save me before it was too late.

The new millennium marked a new start for Douglas and me. He left the RAF, receiving a healthy amount in severance pay, and quickly found work for a civilian company. I also found an enjoyable new job as a communication support worker at a local college for students studying an IT foundation course.

My relationships with my children, however, were more problematic. Alex was still smoking cannabis, but I had reason to hope that he would one day find the answers he was looking for. Just 18 months or so before, he had asked to come home, as he wanted a break, and I felt myself take a deep breath as I saw my son. He looked haggard and somehow small, which is difficult for a big man. He must have noticed the concern on my face, as he explained that as a devotee of the club scene he had been using Ecstasy on a regular basis and knew he had to somehow break the cycle he was caught up in. All I wanted to do was hold him and make it better, and for the next few weeks he rested while I fed him up on home cooking. Gradually, his gaunt features began to fill out.

He then managed to secure a job with a local company, and I was so pleased to see his confidence increase by the day until he was ready to start his life afresh again. Alex was now settled in the north of England, with a job he enjoyed, and I looked forward to his occasional visits. For a while now he had been talking about going backpacking, and I encouraged him, as I never wanted any of my children to feel they didn't have the right to chase their dreams.

Heidi had by now separated from Nat and was living alone with the children down in Somerset. There were elements of her life that angered and saddened me by turns, as I was aware she was involved with some undesirable people. Drink and drugs had begun to feature, and this caused me great concern not only for her sake but also for that of my grandchildren. Whenever I raised the subject, though, I ran the risk of incurring her wrath, and many of our old tensions had begun to resurface. With hindsight, I would have to say they had never really been resolved, so it was not going to take much to light the touchpaper.

I was aware that Megan also still harboured a level of resentment towards me concerning my break-up with Dave and the subsequent hostilities, and this served to make our relationship somewhat volatile. She was happy in a stable relationship with her partner, though, and I was deeply moved when she asked me to be present at the birth of her first child in the spring of 2001. I love all of my grandchildren as equally as I do dearly, but I had never had the joy of being present at a birth before, as we had always been overseas. The delivery was by no means straightforward, and at one crucial point my heart was in my mouth as I paced the corridors praying I would not lose Megan or her little baby. For once my prayers were answered, and I was privileged enough to hold little Holly in my arms when she was just a few minutes old. I would like to think this moment, which I shall cherish for ever, has forged a close and everlasting bond between both of our hearts.

The start of the college's summer vacation in July that year found me at a loose end, so I was delighted when Megan asked me if I would like to stay and help her with Holly. As Douglas was away on business in America for the next fortnight, it seemed the ideal opportunity to spend some quality time with my mum, children and grandchildren. I was under no illusions that this would be a straightforward happy family reunion, though, as relations were somewhat strained between Heidi and me, as they were between the two sisters, but nothing could have prepared me for what was to happen.

I was really looking forward to seeing my granddaughter Lucy perform in her end-of-term school play one afternoon, and I knew Heidi was equally excited at the prospect of us both being there to witness it. On the morning of the play, Megan expressed an interest in joining us, and it warmed my heart to think we could all attend as a family. I rang Heidi straightaway to see if perhaps she might like to join Megan and me for lunch prior to the show, and I couldn't help but notice the forced indifference in her voice as she declined the offer on the grounds that she was too busy.

As Megan drove us back from our meal, we spotted Heidi coming out of her house, and Megan pulled over to speak with her sister. I didn't hear the initial exchange, but an argument started between them almost immediately, and Megan and I drove off to her flat. A short while later, the bell rang and in marched Heidi. I was sitting with my back to the pair of them at the kitchen table, holding baby Holly in my arms. I tensed as I heard their row resume, and as tempers quickly flared, Megan asked her sister to leave in no uncertain terms. Sensing the situation was far from resolved, I stood with the baby in my arms and asked Heidi to leave before something happened that we might all regret. In an instant, Heidi switched her attack to me with such venom it took my breath away. I'd seen Heidi's rage in full flow before, so I recognised all the signs, but already I knew this was the most intense anger I had ever witnessed in her, and I quickly passed the baby to Megan. My protective instincts told me it was imperative to get Heidi out of the flat as soon as possible, and I tried to edge her to the door at the top of the landing, all the while her face remaining just inches from mine as her invective flowed and I screamed back in retaliation. She accused me of never wanting or loving her, and threw in my face all the men that I had brought into her life and the different places I had dragged her around. At the time, I was too angry to realise that she had a point, and instead I challenged her about her own abilities as a mother. It was then that she raised her fist.

My remaining strength was all but spent as she relentlessly beat me into submission, but then suddenly she was knocked from me by Megan, who appeared to just fly over the top of me. For a moment, the girls exchanged a flurry of blows, and then it ceased as suddenly as it had started when Heidi bolted for the door, which I, running on sheer adrenalin, struggled to lock behind her. Megan and I clung to each other for a while in stunned disbelief at what had just happened. It seemed like we had survived some nightmare, but the searing pain in my head and body reminded me it had been all too real. When the police arrived, I decided there and then to press charges, as something needed to be done to make Heidi take control of her temper. She had to be forced to take responsibility for her actions once and for all, before something even worse happened.

My head felt strange for days to follow, and my vision was affected. My arms and legs were black and blue, and I was swollen all over, but the real pain came from the recurring images of Heidi's contorted face and her cruel words. These images in turn evoked older memories that had lain dormant for years. I remembered the taunts that Ronald had directed at me and felt that I must truly be the evil person he had always said I was for my own flesh and blood to turn on me in this way. I must have deserved the beating my daughter had meted out to me as punishment for my sins. Such notions dominated my thoughts for weeks to come, and for the most part I couldn't stop crying.

At the end of August, I returned to college to help the new students enrol, but from the first day back I was aware that I was not functioning properly. I could not recall phone messages long enough to write them down, I had problems hearing and following what the lecturers were saying, and my concentration had been shot to pieces. I returned home in tears, as I was aware something was acutely wrong, and when the next day followed the same course, I consulted my doctor to see if he could help. He told me I was still suffering from concussion of the ear, which explained my hearing loss, the buzzing noise in my head and the continuous bouts of nausea and dizziness, but I was now also starting to suffer blackouts. I could be driving along when suddenly a near-miss would wake me from my half-sleep, only for me to realise I had absolutely no recollection of the past 10 or 15 minutes.

On a trip to the supermarket, I couldn't help but wince and duck as a man reached across me to take something from the shelf, and my ear-splitting scream as I fell to the floor led to people staring at me from all directions as if I had some dreadful illness. A young lady came forward to help me to my feet, as I was trembling from head to toe. I heard the man repeatedly say he hadn't touched me, but I was unable to open my mouth to speak – it was as if I was removed in some way from the whole incident. I was escorted to the manager's office, where I explained that I was all right and that the man had only reached over me. I made my apologies over and over again as I declined their offer to call a doctor. I just wanted to get back to the safety of my own home as soon as possible.

On other occasions, it was frustration rather than fear that enveloped me, such as one time in town when a young man tried to pull out in front of me in his car. I simply saw red, so I refused to let him enter the flow of traffic. I sat there gripping the steering wheel, muttering that I would not be pushed around any more; I would not be bullied by him or anyone else. The thud of his outstretched hand slamming the side of my car as I passed shattered my illusion, and by the time I got home I was once more a quivering, sobbing wreck. Following this incident, I was signed off work, as I no longer wanted to leave the house. I felt as if the whole world was closing in on me, and my daughter's assault on me replayed constantly in my head. I began to suffer frequent, severe panic attacks, and as I struggled to inflate my lungs with rasping breaths, I wished death would come and bring me the release I craved.

Douglas was painfully aware, as I was, that I desperately needed help, and when my doctor referred me to a psychiatrist, Douglas used the private health care his company offered to get a quick referral to the Priory Hospital.

TWENTY-FOUR

Laid to Rest

It all made perfect sense now that I could see clearly. The faces of my mum, husband, children and grandchildren flashed before my eyes, and I was convinced that if I died, they would all be a lot happier without me. Throughout my life I have had suicidal thoughts in times of emotional difficulty, and I had made attempts to take my own life before without success. Now, after only my second week of attending the Priory as an outpatient, I found similar notions forming in my mind. That afternoon, as I sat in the group session, I didn't hear a word that was said, for all I could see in my mind was my new life slipping away. Ronald had won in the end. They all had. I could not continue to live with the knowledge that my daughter hated me so much, and this time I had an exit plan that would not fail.

Then, just as the session was drawing to a close, something from the deepest recesses inside me stirred and came rushing to the forefront of my mind to clear all thoughts of my own demise. It was quite simply the will to live. I didn't want to die; I wanted to clear away the shadow that had been hanging over me since childhood. At the end of the session, I asked to speak with the group leader, and when everyone had left I broke down and told her what I had been planning for weeks and explained that I was very frightened of what I might do to myself. I was referred to a doctor, and it was agreed that I should be admitted to the hospital as an inpatient the very next day. Part of me felt I had failed, as I had been unable to cope on my own, but another part of me recognised that this course of action was the only one left open to me and that I was very lucky to be receiving such expert help.

I would spend the best part of a year in their care, two months of which were as an inpatient. At first I wasn't in the mood to cooperate, as I just didn't have the energy. Gradually, however, I began to respond and open up about not only the confrontation between Heidi and myself but also some of the underlying issues regarding my birth-father, which I wrongly thought I had addressed fully during my session with the psychiatric nurse who had counselled me years before. Having finally managed to give the consultants a fuller picture, I was eventually diagnosed as suffering from clinical depression and post-traumatic stress disorder. At the time these terms meant little to me; all I knew was that I had a room in my mind that I had tried to keep closed for so many years, a section from which images of people and faces, sounds and smells were increasingly screaming for my attention. There were some that I recognised whilst others were the vaguest of outlines, but they were there nonetheless and they were not going to go away on their own. Under the guidance of the medical team, these half-hidden memories were beginning to come to the fore; some poured thick and fast whilst others merely trickled, and they all had the power to trigger other memories, both good and bad.

Patients were checked night and day to make sure they were coping, but the frequency of such checks depended on how long a patient had been there and the state of their progress. Patients were not assigned specific staff; the shifts would change and so would the faces of those monitoring us. One evening, my head was throbbing with the influx of partially formed images from the past when the shard of light from the half-opened door disrupted my contemplation. All I could make out in the half-light was the face of a black man and his round glasses glinting in the light. In an instant, I felt the panic take over and reality was submerged in a tidal wave of vivid memories washing over me from all directions. It was as if I had been sucked backwards into the past, and it was now all there with me in the room itself, literally pushing me out of my bed and forcing me into the room's darkest corner, where I hoped to find sanctuary from the violent images.

It was there the nurse found me, and in a torrent of tears the events of the gang rape all those years before came flooding out. It was the first time in my life I acknowledged to myself the fact that I had actually been raped, and in turn had it acknowledged by someone else that I had been the victim and was not to blame for the ordeal I'd suffered. To have that reassurance felt like a soothing balm being poured over me from above, easing the pain that I had carried for so long.

With the expert guidance of the Priory staff, I now began to unravel and reveal more of my past, learning new ways of dealing with the panic attacks these sessions invariably evoked. It was as if I were being led all the way back to my childhood so I could console the child within me for all of the unresolved traumas, thus enabling me to move on as an adult. This regression did, however, make my return home each weekend rather difficult, as just going out on my own or into shops crowded with people became an ordeal. The biggest achievement I made during that time was actually returning to Megan's flat and the scene of Heidi's vicious assault. The first visit was particularly difficult as I struggled to cope with vivid images of Heidi's fury, and in the following months I had only so much as to see a picture of her or hear her name mentioned and that familiar panic would begin to rise in me.

The Priory staff had shown me methods to tone down these anxiety attacks, though, and I knew the only way I could really come to terms with these feelings was to face them head-on. This I achieved by taking up Megan's request to help her decorate the flat. I threw myself into the work, spending every spare moment there alone in a bid to force myself to confront my demons, and gradually I came to realise the roots of these fears lay not only in the assault itself but in the fact that it had opened the floodgates to all my private torments. In a strange way, I therefore had reason to be grateful to Heidi. She had been visited by the police after the assault but, as the sympathetic inspector whom I met after the attack informed me it was unlikely to proceed to court, she was given a caution and a severe warning about what would happen to her in the future if anything similar occurred again. I could only hope that she had learnt something from this horrendous experience.

Having enjoyed a wonderful New Year's celebration in Lancashire with Douglas's mother and father, I checked the phone messages on our return. There was the usual assortment, until the final message played. The voice was that of the head of the home where Ronald had been staying, and she said she was sorry to inform me that Ronald had passed away. I had always said I would dance on his grave when he died, yet when I heard the news, there was no elation, no sadness or sense of loss, nothing but relief, for I was now free and so was he. I did not attend the funeral, as it would have been hypocritical to have made some show of grief for this man; my only grief was for the abstract notion of the natural father I'd never had.

I was beginning to learn that the past had its place, and it was neither in the present nor the future if I ever wanted to achieve the level of contentment and happiness I craved. But while this was all well and good in theory, it was a little harder to put into practice. I was aware that Megan had been trying behind the scenes to help heal the rift between Heidi and me, and I could hear Heidi in the background when Megan called one evening to say her sister wished to talk to me. Initially, I resisted, as I didn't feel sufficiently prepared to speak with Heidi yet, but I promised Megan I would consider it and call her back if I felt up to it. Within an hour or so, my fingers were trembling as I dialled Megan's number, then waited for her to call her sister to the phone.

Heidi's words of apology for what she had done were

welcome, but didn't register immediately as it was all I could do to stave off the flashbacks the sound of her voice had brought on, and we ended the conversation cordially if somewhat frostily. We spoke by phone on a few occasions after this, thawing the ice piece by piece as we chatted about the grandchildren, but it was very difficult for us both. I was aware that Heidi suffered with dreadful guilt over what she had done to me; I was not the only one who had been reliving that day over and over ever since.

I was not without guilt of my own, as I couldn't deny that there was a good deal of truth in the words that Heidi had hurled at me that day. She had spent her early childhood being dragged along behind me as I ricocheted from one failed relationship to the next, and I had never given a great deal of thought to the effect that this might have on her and, later, the other children. At the time, I was so consumed with my own problems that I concentrated on taking care of Heidi's physical needs – making sure she was well fed and dressed – but I neglected her emotional needs, until she forced me to take notice of her through bad behaviour. I had resented my own birth-mother for failing to save me from Ronald's abuse, but could I honestly look at my own daughter and not acknowledge that I had failed her too? I had in fact failed them all.

I was still helping Megan decorate her flat, and one day as I was busy tiling her bathroom, Heidi's children suddenly entered the room. My delight at seeing them was tempered by the realisation that Heidi must be in the car outside, too apprehensive to make the first move and face me again. After chatting with James, Lucy and

Thomas for a while, I knew I could put it off no longer and asked James to go downstairs and see if his mummy would like to come up. I had not seen Heidi for nearly a year, but she was still my daughter and I loved her regardless of what she had done to me. Even so, as she entered the flat, my pulse-rate soared. Heidi was clearly equally uncomfortable, for neither of us had the courage to look the other in the eye, and the tiling proved to be a useful diversion as I focused all my attention on the job in hand in a bid to hold my nerve. The meeting was as brief as it was tense, with few words spoken on either side, but at least it had paved the way for us to progress, and subsequent meetings became less and less stressful.

Douglas, however, expressed his own reservations about my renewed contact with Heidi. He had no wish to prolong the rift between me and my daughter, but his prime concern was for my welfare, and he was not entirely convinced of Heidi's motives for reconciliation or that she would not hurt me again. I appreciated his concerns, but I felt we had to at least try.

In a roundabout way, Douglas would unfortunately be proved right, as the stress of the situation eventually left me back at the Priory, burnt out and desperate. Fortunately, though, this proved to be merely a temporary blip in my progress, as with the help of my therapist, I learnt it was all right to feel the way I did. I would continue to take steps both backwards and forwards on my long and winding road to recovery.

It was during these sessions that I was also finally able to recount the events of my time at the approved school, and seeing them from a different perspective enabled me to feel secure enough to apply for copies of the official records from my time in care. When the files arrived, I was full of trepidation about what information they would hold and what secrets they might reveal about my life from all those years ago. I took myself away to my room, took a deep breath and ripped open the large manilla envelope; however, the biggest surprise these notes held in store was just how little information they contained. I felt a mixture of emotions on discovering this but mostly anger at social services. They had made vital decisions that had altered the course of my life, and yet it now appeared they had not been important enough to those involved to keep a record of any substance. I cried, shouted and raged at my lost childhood, the years of immense pain and heartache, and I pondered long and hard over whether or not I should make a formal complaint. Ultimately, I consoled myself with the knowledge that all the perpetrators were either dead, like Ronald, or so old they too would soon have to account elsewhere for their sins. At least I now had the choice to leave the past behind where it belonged.

The path to future happiness is rarely signposted for anyone, and my own opened up for me quite unexpectedly during a holiday in the Lake District with Douglas. From the moment we entered the small village where we now live, its warmth embraced me like a favourite blanket on a chilly winter's day, and when Douglas and I set eyes on a small cottage for sale, I knew instinctively, despite its need for extensive renovations, that we had found our new home. I had not felt at ease in our current hometown since the assault. I was all too aware of the noise and any aggressive behaviour, and felt that I needed to escape to the peace and calm of the countryside.

Douglas and I were sure in our own minds that the move north was the right one for us, and thankfully our families were equally supportive. Alex was due to embark on a backpacking trip to the Far East, and he reminded me that I should follow my dreams, just as I had encouraged him to do. The girls were also enthusiastic, although I suspected Megan feared she might not be able to cope without us close to hand when life became difficult for her. While it was hard telling Megan, whom I can't help but still think of as my baby, telling my dear mum was by far the most difficult. She had only to ask us to stay and I'm sure we would have done so, but instead she told me to grasp hold of my dreams with both hands to ensure that I didn't wake up one day regretting a missed chance of happiness.

She was right: we deserved the opportunity to enjoy this adventure, and in June 2004 we moved to our dream cottage. For the first time in my life, I had found somewhere I wanted to settle down and make friends, free from the ghosts of the past. The downside to the move, though, was that Heidi and I began to lose contact again due to the distance between us, and it seemed easier just to let all the unresolved business between us lie dormant.

That all changed when Douglas and I were driving down to visit his mother recently, and the radio chat show we listened to featured both people who were separated from the ones they loved and those who had never had the chance to resolve their differences. I could feel a lump growing in my throat as I listened to a lady speak of losing her daughter and granddaughter in a car accident some years before; she would have given anything just for one more moment with them, and here Heidi and I were virtually pretending that the other didn't exist.

Shortly afterwards, we travelled down to spend some time with my mum and attend Holly's birthday party, which was held in a hall hired out especially for the occasion. A host of family and friends were there, laughing and enjoying themselves, all except Heidi. Suddenly, I spotted her out of the corner of my eye, sitting on her own at a table on the other side of the room, and I thought my heart would break. She'd previously said that throughout her life she had felt left out and unloved, and in that moment she was the embodiment of that statement. While I might have failed Heidi when she was younger, perhaps I had the opportunity to help her now. Without hesitation, I walked over to her and told her she should be with her family, before taking her hand and walking with her to the other side of the room.

There was no magic wand waved that day to solve all the problems that confront my family. Heidi continues to face challenges in her personal life, and in her failed relationships I cannot help but feel that she is repeating the pattern that I taught her in her early life. Alex and Megan have their own issues, and the three of them are not as close as I had hoped when I had my dreams of creating the perfect little family. My own problems with post-traumatic stress disorder return periodically, and even to this day they are occasionally bigger than I am, but for the most part I can control this. Finally, however, despite the traumatic nature of the events that acted as a catalyst, I have been able to confront my past and tell the truth about what happened to me. I have forgiven Heidi for the assault, which in a strange way might actually have saved me. I love her without question and I can only hope that all of my children can forgive me for the effects my life has undoubtedly had on them. Ronald Baird stole my innocence and ruined my childhood, but I refuse to let him ruin my life. His actions cast a shadow over my life and that of my children, but now we have to move on. For one thing I am absolutely certain of is that it was never my children's shame, and now at last I no longer consider it mine.

Epilogue

This book evolved from a number of diary entries written over the past 20 years, as, for me, writing was a form of therapy, a way of acknowledging the past and detaching the fact from the emotion. Although my husband knew of my past, he did not know all of the details, and learning to trust him enough to let him into my darkest places was the final part of my journey.

After reading *Just A Boy* by Richard McCann, I felt compelled to contact him, as the honest way he'd told his own story touched my very soul and gave me inspiration. Although our stories are so different, many of the emotions expressed are the same, and his account of all that he had been through made me feel as if I too could hold my head high and look others in the eye; that I no longer had to carry the shame of another person's actions.

Richard encouraged me to compile my diaries into a book, and as I finished each chapter, my husband would read it, and I would look into his eyes for the rejection, disgust and revulsion I was certain would follow. Instead, each time he would hold me and we would cry together. It felt like stepping into a shower and coming out clean, all my years of shame finally being washed away. My fears of losing my husband proved unfounded, as it has made us stronger than we have ever been.

As I read it back, I found it hard to believe this had been my life, so how could I expect anyone else to believe me and not judge me? When I sent the manuscript to Richard, that was the first time anyone other than my husband would read in detail what had happened to me. He felt my story deserved to be told and put me in touch with Robert Potter, a writer I could very quickly see would take my life story and treat it with great care. He understood my reasons for writing it, not for gain or to point fingers but to show that childhood abuse affects more people than just the victim; it affects everyone connected to the victim, whilst the perpetrator walks away, more often than not without prosecution and oblivious to the damage he or she has caused.

These perpetrators go on to harm again and again because of the fear and shame they instil in both their victims and their families. As a result of denial or ignorance, or simply as a means of survival, families can turn against a victim; they close ranks in a bid to block out the truth, thus leaving the victim to feel abused and raped all over again. The perpetrator's act therefore causes a negative ripple on the water, but for every person who stands up and tells his or her story, a positive ripple is caused to counter it. I therefore cannot thank Bill Campbell of Mainstream Publishing enough for seeing the worth of my story and giving me the chance to be heard. The rape conviction is 5 per cent in England and 4.3 per cent in Scotland, so it is only through awareness, education and changes in the law to protect the innocent that we can ever hope to change society's attitudes to rape and abuse. It is my dearest hope that this book will allow me to reach out to others in pain and give them hope, for they too can choose to be a survivor.

Sources of Support for Survivors of Abuse and Rape

Rape crisis centres provide free and confidential support to women and girls who have experienced sexual violence, no matter when or how. Centres are based throughout the UK and Ireland. As well as offering support to survivors of sexual violence, the rape crisis movement works to raise awareness of sexual violence, and to challenge attitudes that blame women for the violence inflicted upon them. For details of your local Rape Crisis Centre, contact:

Rape Crisis Scotland: 0141 248 8848;
www.rapecrisisscotland.org.uk

Rape Crisis Network Ireland: 1800 778888;
www.rcni.ie

Rape Crisis Network UK: info@rapecrisis.org.uk;
www.rapecrisis.org.uk

NAPAC is the National Association for People Abused in Childhood (Registered Charity No. 1069802). They provide a national freephone support line and a postal and e-mail service offering support and advice for people who have experienced emotional, sexual or physical abuse and/or neglect in childhood.

Support line: 0800 085 3330; www.napac.org.uk